Exit Narratives

Reflections of Four
Retired Teachers

Nathalis G. Wamba
Ursula Foster
Elena Davis
Jackquelynn Jones
Barbara Storck

UNIVERSITY PRESS OF AMERICA,® INC.
Lanham • Boulder • New York • Toronto • Plymouth, UK

Copyright © 2010 by
University Press of America,® Inc.
4501 Forbes Boulevard
Suite 200
Lanham, Maryland 20706
UPA Acquisitions Department (301) 459-3366

Estover Road
Plymouth PL6 7PY
United Kingdom

Library of Congress Control Number: 2010922963
ISBN: 978-0-7618-5115-8 (paperback : alk. paper)
eISBN: 978-0-7618-5116-5

Contents

Acknowledgments

I want to thank my co-authors. Without them this book would never have happened. They showed dedication, commitment and perseverance for a project that took five years. I take this opportunity to acknowledge their combined experience of about a century in the New York public school system and how privileged I was to join their conversations during which they attempted to sort out issues, reflect on their experiences, disagreeing with each other at times always hoping that their insights might be of use to future generations of teachers.

A special thanks to Ursula who offered her apartment as the venue of our monthly meetings. She served us breakfast and took care of the scheduling and logistics and made sure that all of us felt very comfortable.

Several people read this manuscript and offered constructive feedback. We are indebted to Samantha Jory Deutch, Johanna Foster, John Golden, Winthrop Holder, Carrie Lewis John-Ayi, Ellen Levy, Mark Mackintosh, Terry Quinn, Kerfe Roig-Irwin, Ronna Texidor and Anita Palathingal, our manuscript editor. We must, of course, absolve them of any responsibility for errors or for opinions with which they still disagree. Each of them saved us from embarrassing errors and challenged our thinking in crucial ways.

Finally, we thank our parents, our children, our partners and friends who encouraged us to take on this project as it burgeoned from discussions over bagels and coffee to co-authoring a book.

Introduction

Women who chose to teach have a rich tradition on which to draw for guidance and inspiration.

Nancy Hoffman

Books on education theories abound. However, it is in the classroom where theory meets practice and vice versa. We wrote this book to examine what constitutes good teaching and engaged learning and how to use this knowledge to support teachers in their efforts to create learning environments that encourage academic mastery and nourish students as social beings. Too often dedicated teachers who have changed the lives of so many children lack the opportunity to reflect on their classroom experiences from which other teachers might benefit.

My coauthors—retired teachers from the New York public school system with a combined experience of about a century—have used the writing of this book as a means of reflecting on what they have done in their classrooms, what it meant to be a competent, creative, and caring teacher. They share what they taught, learned, and experienced with a constant reference to the needs and the hopes of their students.

This project began one morning in 2004 after Ursula, an elementary school teacher with over two decades of experience, had just returned from Uganda where she spent two years as a Peace Corps volunteer.

Ursula's trip to Uganda greatly impacted her. Unlike many Americans, who after a short trip to Central Africa make pronouncements on what Africans need to do to develop their countries, Ursula shared her joys about working in a different culture where she felt embraced by the people, speaking Luganda and negotiating life in dire socioeconomic conditions. She spoke about what she learned from the people and what she struggled to contribute.

We talked about education in Uganda and New York City. Ursula spoke about how things had drastically changed in the New York City public school system since her return from Uganda. The mayor of New York City had taken control of the Board of Education and renamed it the Department of Education and appointed a non educator as chancellor.

The No Child Left Behind Act (NCLB), signed into law January 8, 2002, by President Bush, altered the public education system throughout the country. It represented an unprecedented increase in the role that the federal government played in education. The core mandate of the law requires states to (a) ensure that highly qualified teachers are in every classroom, (b) use research-based practices as the foundation of instruction, (c) develop tests to assess students so that data-driven decisions become an integral part of the educational system, and (d) hold schools accountable for the performance of all students (Yell & Drascow, 2005).

Who could possibly disagree with these reasonable mandates? At a conference on reducing the achievement gap in the school system, a keynote speaker commented, I paraphrase, "For all the fuss about No Child Left Behind, let us at least acknowledge the fact that, for the first time, teachers are being held accountable about what takes place in the classroom. I do not think that this is such a bad thing." This speaker, however, neglected to discuss the threat rigidity imposed on teachers and students by this legislation. Staw, Sandelands, and Dutton (1981) explain that threat rigidity is the theory that an organization, when perceiving itself under siege (threatened or in crisis) responds in identifiable ways: structures tighten, centralized control increases, conformity is stressed, accountability and efficiency measures are emphasized, and alternative or innovative thinking is discouraged (Olsen et al., 2009).

The changes imposed by the NCLB frustrated Ursula, who worked from a commitment to stimulate critical thinking, practical life skills and constructive social engagement. I asked her how she intended to handle this change. "I am planning to retire" she answered. Her response shocked me because I never expected her to retire this early. "I do not know what I am going to do. I have to think about it" she continued. The No Child Left Behind legislation took the enthusiasm out of her work.

In my attempt to help her think of something to do I suggested that she gather a group of retired teachers who would be interested in reflecting collectively on their careers as teachers in the New York public school system. I explained that such a group would have a great deal to say about the changes that were taking place in the public school system. More importantly, their reflections could be of great value to future generations of teachers and policy makers, should they choose to write about it.

"Good idea!" Ursula replied. "I will ask a group of colleagues who retired last year and this year if they would be interested and I will let you know." A month later, I received a phone call from Ursula telling me that she had talked to six retired teachers and one school social worker who were interested in the idea.

On October 8, 2004, I met them in her apartment. They all seemed enthusiastic about the chance to discuss and evaluate their many decades of commitment to teaching and learning. At a time when the New York City public school system was experiencing a serious teachers' shortage, I wondered why all of these teachers were retiring. Fifteen thousand had retired between 2001 and 2004.

As a newcomer to the group, I wanted to establish good rapport and build trust. Being an academic carries liabilities. One of the teachers asked me, "Are you writing a paper on this or what?" Ursula quickly replied, "No! He already has his Ph.D." The question gave me the opportunity to introduce myself and explain what Ursula and I discussed when we first talked about this project. I explained that we wanted to get together a group of retired teachers and have them reflect on their experiences, articulate what they had learned from their work in the New York City public schools system, describe how they navigated such a complex educational system, explain how they became competent teachers, specifically what made them successful, discuss the challenges they encountered and what kept them going and, finally, to offer some advice to young men and women who want to become teachers.

Once I explained the purpose of our project, the group embarked in a free flow conversation about their experiences. No specific structure directed the conversation. It unfolded sometimes as conversation, and sometimes as brainstorming. The discussion focused on topics that included; why go into teaching; the first year of teaching; anger, sadness, and joy; not a nine-to-five job; labor union issues; teaching history; school reform; curriculum areas; the teaching community; supervision; connections between school and students' families and community; the role and impact of principals; students' needs and desires and the time required to develop the craft of teaching. We agreed to meet once a month to discuss one topic at a time.

The beginning turned out to be rough. Our meetings amounted to cathartic sessions. The members expressed anger. Most of them had left the system not because they wanted to, but in protest against what they experienced as an extremely narrow-minded education policy. They spoke about how the climate of standardization, conformity, and high-stakes testing ignored their training, talent, artistry, and skills as educators. And, more importantly, they reacted to an educational policy that dismissed their contribution to the lives of thousands of children they cherished. Other educational scholars have begun to examine similar forms of teacher anger and disillusionment brought on by the strictures of increased focus on accountability and high stake-testing. Sonia Nieto (2003) writes, "Baffled by school policies that are made by people far removed from the daily realities of classroom life, indignant at being treated as if they were children. I was surprised by the depth of anger of the teachers in the inquiry group."

These free flow conversations lasted for a year. In the process, some of the group members could no longer continue for one reason or another. Three members left us. The core group of Barbara, Elena, Jackquelynn, and Ursula began to crystallize. It became apparent to them that they could not cover all the topics that they wanted to examine. I suggested that we focus our conversations on specific topics we felt strongly about and examine them in depth.

From a long list of topics, the group members decided to select six topics, including; why go into teaching; the first year of teaching; becoming a competent teacher; what worked; the last year of teaching; and the first year out. However, nothing was decided yet. This list changed many times as our conversations progressed.

During the first year, I recorded all the conversations. The second year, the group members contributed funds to transcribe the tapes. I suggested to them that they use the transcripts and start writing about topics of interest to them. We still were uncertain about what the final product would look like.

Elena suggested to the group that they each write accounts on a given topic in separate voices. The only requirement was to bring the writing to our meeting and share it with the group members.

Reading the pieces aloud became a ritual. I collected each and every piece of writing. A surprise degree of commonality emerged in these writings. The group members wrote about similar observations and practices. Some of the anecdotes were even identical. This occurred because I believe that the development of the craft of teaching shares some common elements and realizations.

Writing expanded the project. It forced the group members to develop their thoughts and react to each other's stories. Sonia Nieto (2003) writes, "Writing about teaching, especially if they share their writing with colleagues, is a public way of understanding and improving their work."

MY ROLE

"The teaching profession is full of people who do not respect its purposes. If teaching is to become vital and honorable again, it is teachers who will have to make it so. It is the voice of the teacher that must at last be heard," writes

William Ayers (1993). This quote, and my experience as a graduate student working as a tutor and mentor in some of the worst New York City high schools, motivated me to initiate this project.

I met dedicated teachers and school administrators, and excellent students. I also encountered teachers who did not belong in the school system. On one occasion, a teacher told me, "The best way to hide something from these kids is to put it on the board." Spending time in teachers' lounges yielded a variety of insights about education, school, students, and teachers. I was privileged to witness some narratives we seldom hear.

I wanted to promote reflection among teachers, but also to facilitate the access of a broader public to those reflections. Ursula, Elena, Jackie, and Barbara had accumulated many decades of experience working as teachers. This project offered an opportunity for a collective reflection on their careers as teachers.

We engaged in democratic conversations about education. I suggested a round robin style that gave each individual the opportunity to contribute and be heard. Experiences and insights varied and added to the richness of the picture that was emerging. This process taught us to listen to each other carefully, to probe and to push each others' thinking further.

All ideas found currency in our conversations. Censorship was verboten. The group opened up to a variety of perspectives in such a way that no one could assume to have a monopoly on the truth. We all were engaged in this learning process, willing to be surprised and even proven wrong.

This predisposition allowed a firm understanding of the various issues on the table. The group challenged assumptions, for example, that all children can learn. Indeed, all children can learn. However, under what conditions? The process was sometimes tedious, demanding, confusing, and unclear. Sometimes, the group surprised itself when new ways of looking at a situation emerged, an unexpected pattern of thinking emerged and lent to the whole process a sense of purpose and possibility.

Last but not least was the idea of creating a community of teachers who had worked in the school system before and after the imposition of the No Child Left Behind legislation on the public school system. They were willing to break their silence and share what they had learned, to challenge the system, and to speak without fear of any retribution.

PLAN OF THIS BOOK

In the first chapter, I discuss the concept of a competent teacher. What does it mean to be a competent, creative, and caring teacher? I reviewed literature to provide a conceptual framework for the reader. I leave it to the reader to decide whether the teachers who share their experiences in this book are competent, creative, and caring.

In the second chapter "Why Me?" My co-authors reflect on why they became teachers; specifically, what motivated them to do so. They talk about the early years when they were in elementary school, where they began to model their teachers' behaviors.

The third chapter, "My First Year Teaching," is about what it is like to step into a classroom for the first time and teach. Each teacher experiences this moment differently. One learns to teach by doing, trying, failing, retrying, and succeeding.

The fourth chapter examines how they became confident teachers. "Rome was not built in one day" is Jackquelynn's analogy. Elena points out that it takes at least five to seven years to really get the "aha" moment of knowing what teaching is. It takes a long time, commitment, and the ability to reflect on one's mistakes to become a confident teacher. With confidence, one is more likely to become a good teacher.

The fifth chapter explores what worked for each of these teachers. This is a toolkit for working with children. For Barbara, it was the math lab, for Ursula it was the multiage classroom, the community rituals, and the parents' club, among other things, for Jackquelynn it was the literacy lab, and for Elena it was simple rules of respect, fairness, and consistency.

In the sixth chapter, the group members dissect the relationships between teachers, administrators, parents, and children, and the relationships within these groups. It covers the micropolitics of school communities; the way people coexist with each other; how they compete or cooperate; how teachers treat each other; how they handle issues of race, class, sexual orientation, religion, etc.

The seventh chapter examines the last years of teaching. A lot of tears were shed in the writing of this chapter. The teachers described their last year in the public school, the last song they sang, the kids they left, the bureaucracy they could not abide by, and the education policy that spat on them.

The eighth chapter describes the activities they engaged in after retiring. Jackquelynn traveled to Qatar in the United Arab Emirates and worked as a consultant. While there, she continued working on our project and faithfully emailed us her written pieces. Ursula was managing a small grant foundation, amongst other things. Elena was caring for her beloved, aged mother and her dynamic teenage daughters. In addition, they were all busy working on this book.

The ninth chapter is the conclusion, a summary of the recurring themes throughout the book.

The tenth chapter, a reflection, addresses the main themes that emerged during our conversations: the children, teaching and education policy.

Sadly, as we neared the end of our project, our dear friend Barbara was diagnosed with cancer. She died in April 2008. Barbara was an active member of our group. We profoundly miss her presence and her contribution to this project.

Chapter One

Competent Teacher

Susan Reynolds (2008), who edited *My Teacher Is My Hero: Tributes to the People Who Gave Us Knowledge, Motivation, and Wisdom*, defines a teacher as anyone—a coach, a music or art teacher, a writing instructor, a mentor, a beloved relative, a close personal friend, an acquaintance, someone you met on a journey, a shaman, a spiritual advisor, a priest, a rabbi. I take from her definition that anyone can be a teacher. However, not everyone can be a school teacher. She further comments that the best teachers are fabulous characters who love what they do and convey enthusiasm for learning, respect and responsibility, and a certain joie de vivre. They believe in the potential of students and will do whatever it takes to unleash it and set it ablaze. Unfortunately, even the best teachers may not receive the accolades they deserve, at least while they are in service. Often their contributions are not recognized until many years later.

How can anyone tell that someone is a good teacher? After teaching for almost twelve years, this question still lingers in my mind. As a college teacher, students evaluate me at the end of each semester. Are these evaluations sufficient to certify me as a good teacher? Maybe or maybe not. There is more to teaching than merely those student evaluations.

There are days when I leave my class excited and feeling that I was able to connect with my students in a special way and inspire them. Other days I feel like running off and burying myself, especially when a course goes pearshape. Experiencing these contradictory moments has taught me that teaching competency is not a matter of years of teaching; it depends upon daily reflection on one's teaching practice. Unless one reflects on what is taking place in a classroom, one cannot achieve competency.

In January 1, 1988, Lindsay Law, an executive producer with Warner Bros. Pictures, produced the movie *Stand and Deliver*, based on the true story of

1

Jaime Escalante, a dedicated East Los Angeles high school teacher who transformed some of his students into math scholars. Jaime Escalante was born in La Paz in Bolivia. While there, he taught physics and mathematics for fourteen years. In 1964, he immigrated to the United States. His first stop was in Puerto Rico, where he enrolled at the Universidad de Puerto Rico to study science and mathematics before moving to California. In California, he soon realized that his English was extremely poor and that he had no teaching credentials in the United States. He enrolled at Pasadena City College, taking English courses in the evening, and went on to earn a degree in electronics. He took a day job and continued studying and earned a mathematics degree.

In 1976 he began teaching at Garfield High School in East Los Angeles, one of the worst high schools in the city. Gangs controlled the school. Despite the odds against him, Jaime Escalante motivated a small group of students to take classes in calculus. He provided constant instruction. He cared about those students and also loved them. More importantly, he believed in their ability to learn calculus. In 1982, his students took the Advanced Placement calculus exam and passed it. The Educational Testing Services, which administered the test, invalidated the scores under the assumption that students had cheated. Most of the students retook the test and passed it.

Today, Jaime Escalante is a national hero and one of the most famous educators in the United States. *Stand and Deliver* became a classic film about American education. In recognition of this incredible achievement, Jaime Escalante received the United States Presidential Medal and the Andres Bello Award by the Organization of American States.

Marva Collins grew up in Atmore, Alabama, during the Jim Crow era. She taught for two years in the public school system after graduating from Clark College in Atlanta, Georgia. She then moved to Chicago where she taught in the public school system for fourteen years. Dissatisfied with the Chicago public school system and the quality of education her two young children were receiving in a prestigious private school, she decided that children deserved better than what was passing for acceptable education.

She took the $5,000 balance in her school pension fund and opened a school on the second floor of her home. She enrolled her two children and four neighborhood youngsters. She founded the Westside Preparatory School in 1975, in Garfield Park, a Chicago inner city area. She took in children with all kinds of problems, even a child who was labeled borderline retarded by the school authorities in the Chicago public school system.

At the end of the first year, every child scored at least five grades higher, proving that the previous labels placed on them were wrong. The CBS television program *60 Minutes* visited the school twice. On the second visit in 1996, the CBS crew learned that the little girl who was labeled borderline mentally retarded graduated from college summa cum laude. Marva's graduates have entered some of the nation's finest colleges and universities such as Harvard, Yale, Princeton, and Stanford, to name just a few.

Marva Collins received many accolades for her work and was featured on *Good Morning America*, *20/20*, Fox News, and many other TV and radio programs. A made-for-television movie entitled *The Marva Collins Story* first aired in 1982 and is still shown on television. Marva received several awards including The Jefferson Award for Benefiting the Disadvantaged, the Humanitarian Award for Excellence, the Legendary Women of the World Award, many honorary doctoral degrees from universities such as Amherst, Dartmouth, Notre Dame, and Clark University, and the prestigious National Humanities Medal from President Bush in 2004.

There are many more master teachers who remain unsung heroes. Accomplished teachers do not always present themselves wrapped in neat and predictable packages. In fact, some of them evoke strong and sometimes negative feelings. They may not have received the media publicity that Escalante or Collins received. Nevertheless, they have changed lives, and their students bear witness to the fact.

What made Escalante and Collins memorable? Historian Richard Traina (1999) examined the autobiographies of 125 prominent Americans from the nineteenth and twentieth centuries, paying attention to the description these leaders gave of the teachers they admired the most in their lives. The descriptions these leaders gave were remarkably consistent. Excellent teachers showed a command of the subject matter; they cared deeply about their students, and their teaching style exhibited a distinctive attribute. These are discussed below.

KNOWLEDGE OF THE SUBJECT MATTER, CURIOSITY, AND AWARENESS

For those who are still arguing whether teaching is an art or a science, I subscribe to the idea that it is both. There is a scientific aspect to teaching; from the Latin word *scientia*, which means knowledge. Shulman (1987) identified seven kinds of knowledge effective teachers must have: knowledge of content, classroom management and organization, curriculum materials and programs, teaching of particular topics, knowledge about the students, knowledge about the educational context, ranging from the classroom group to the community, and knowledge about educational aims and values. McEwan (2002) summarized these traits into three concepts: book learning, street smarts, and mental life. Book learning is knowledge based on the accumulated literature and studies in a content area, as well as the historical and philosophical scholarship on the nature of knowledge in that content area. Street smart teachers know their students, the school, and the community in which they are teaching. They also know the rules, the language, and the culture of the students and parents with whom they work. They use this knowledge to solve problems in the instructional settings. Effective teachers possess the ability to read their own mental state and assess how it affects their present and future performance (mental life). They have the ability to think aloud and model strategic learning for students. They reflect on their teaching behaviors for the purpose of self-growth, and articulate ideas, issues, beliefs, and values about the act of teaching with colleagues, students, and parents. Last, they are flexible to the changing needs and demands of the profession.

Gary Griffin (1999) from Teachers College comments on the traditional expectations for teachers that include a solid academic understanding of the discipline, a repertoire of teaching strategies, a disposition to work solely for the benefit of the students, rather than for oneself, clear and high expectations for students, knowledge and skill related to student assessment, capability in curriculum work, and the like. Teaching involves simultaneous, decision-related content, pedagogy, student relationships, materials of instructions, and interactions with colleagues and others. Managing this complexity amounts to a serious challenge. Griffin states that teacher education program must provide teachers with an opportunity to analyze, reflect, and try out a variety of ways of working well in a complicated social and intellectual environment.

As a baseline, a teacher sets goals taking into account the information or skills he or she wants students to master. The teacher designs learning experiences and scaffolds them in such a way that new experiences build on previous ones and promote learning growth. Lastly, a teacher must evaluate whether the learning intended in the classroom has occurred, and if not, assess the kind of learning that took place, since learning always happens.

Another key factor teachers must consider is the changing nature of knowledge. Curiosity and an awareness of knowledge change must guide the teaching and learning process. This suggests that a teacher must commit to lifelong learning. By becoming a lifelong learner, a teacher will likely discover methods and strategies that will unlock the learning, emotional, and behavioral problems of his or her students. Deep teaching knowledge includes knowledge about the ways of representing and presenting content in order to foster learning or the construction of meaningful understanding (Einhardt et al. 1991).

KNOWLEDGE OF THE STUDENTS

An Alaskan proverb goes, "You cannot teach me if you do not know me." Dan Rather of CBS News wrote, "The dream begins with a teacher who believes in you." Knowledge of the student precedes teaching effectiveness (cited in Reytnolds, 2008). Lisa Delpit (1995) introduced the idea of teachers as cultural translators for students who struggle to understand the sometimes "foreign" ways of American public schools. She acknowledges the voices of minority teachers and students who have been alienated by the schools' inhospitable ways to non-Anglo cultures.

Children bring to school a social and cultural capital which is the sum of their knowledge, background, dispositions, and skills passed from one generation to the next (Bourdieu 1977). MacLeod (1995) comments that upper-middle-class children inherit a cultural capital that is substantially different from working-class children. Schools embody class interests and ideologies and reward the cultural capital of the dominant class. Drawing on Bourdieu's theory of cultural capital, MacLeod writes, "Upper middle class students, by virtue of a certain linguistic and cultural competence acquired through family upbringing, are provided with the means of appropriation for success in school. Children who read books, visit museums, attend concerts, and go to the theater and cinema (or simply grow up in families where these practices are prevalent) acquire a familiarity with the dominant culture that the education system implicitly requires of its students for academic attainment" (p. 14).

To know students means being familiar with the school, the community, the language, and the socioeconomic status and cultural background of the students. It means to be a student of the culture in which one is teaching. William Ayers (1993) writes, "Most teachers want to know more about their students. We want to understand what motivates them and makes them tick, what engages and interests them, and we want to know why they act as they do" (p. 33).

Some teachers argue that one of the best ways to learn about the culture of students is to live in their community. While this is a good idea, it is not always practical. There are children who live in extremely poor neighborhoods and other who live in extreme wealthy neighborhoods. The majority tend to live in middle- and upper-class neighborhoods. Teachers decide where they want to live or where they can afford living and figure out what it takes to know their students.

Ruby Payne (1998) discusses the importance of understanding the hidden rules under which many poor students operate, as well as the necessity of teaching them the rules that will help them succeed in school and at work. Shirley Brice Heath (1983) conducted her research in two poor rural communities in the South. She discovered that the students' ways of doing things in the classrooms reflected the differences in their communities. She helps educators to understand these differences and to translate them into more effective teaching.

Teachers working in affluent communities experience another kind of challenge. The challenge amounts to dealing with in-your-face and helicopter parents who hover around the schools and constantly challenge the teachers' judgment and authority (McEwan 2002).

Knowing students means constantly searching for clues as to who the students are, where they are coming from, and why they behave the way they do. Effective teachers gather information, structure learning tasks, hold high expectations, and gain the trust and respect of their students. They care deeply about them. These teachers put their students' needs for knowledge and empowerment above lofty ambitions, job security, public acclaim, and even personal safety. Effective teachers become students of their students, seeking to understand before they are understood (Covey 1990).

Competent, creative, and caring teachers espouse the pedagogy of the nineteenth century essayist Ralph Waldo Emerson (n.d.): "The secret of education lies in respecting the pupil. It is not for you to choose what he shall know, what he shall do. It is chosen and foreordained, and he only holds the key to his own secret. By your tempering and thwarting and too much governing he may be hindered from his end and kept out of his own. Respect the child. Wait and see the new product of nature." (cited by Metcalfe and Game, 2006, p. 6).

CULTIVATING A DISTINCTIVE PEDAGOGICAL STYLE

There is abundant literature on the mechanics of teaching i.e., effective instructional strategies, effective classroom management strategies, and the use of effective classroom curriculum design strategies. However, research will never be able to identify instructional strategies that work well with every student in every class. The best research can do is to tell us which strategies have a good chance of working well with students. Individual classroom teachers must determine which strategies to employ with students (Marzano 2007).

Commenting on educational research in the 1970s and 1980s, Willms (1992) notes, "I doubt whether another two decades of research will . . . help us specify a model for all seasons—a model that would apply to all schools in all communities at all times." Teddlie and Reynolds (2000) remark, "Sometimes the adoption of ideas from research has been somewhat uncritical; for example, the numerous attempts to apply findings from one specific context to another entirely different context when research has increasingly demonstrated significant contextual differences." (p. 216)

The political context within which teaching and learning occur is often not talked about. Teachers, even when following a predetermined curriculum, make choices about what they are going to teach and how. Paulo Freire (1993) speaking to an audience of several thousands at the California Association for Bilingual Education in Anaheim, California, remarked, "There is no possibility for teaching without learning. As well as there is no possibility of learning without teaching."

Teaching is a political act. The political aspect of teaching manifests itself in the relationship between the students and the teacher. This relationship is imbued with beliefs, assumptions, and preconceived ideas of who is the other. A progressive teacher develops a vision and seeks to understand his or her role in this context and in the world. A progressive teacher is the one whose dreams are fundamentally about rebuilding society, changing reality to create a less ugly society. These are teachers who challenge the status quo and reject the reproductive role of the school (Freire, 1993).

Teacher pedagogy is determined by what students bring to school and how the teacher handles this out-of-school knowledge and life experience. By taking on this teaching challenge, a teacher must realize that to become a good teacher one has to acknowledge that when students come to school, they already know a great deal of things. This is contrary to most teachers who believe that students have nothing to contribute and that they are empty vessels that need to be filled. Before reading the words, the children read the world. The challenge to a progressive teacher is to engage in a dialogue with students and help them share their knowledge so that the teacher can integrate it in the curriculum as a point of reference for the students.

Thus, teaching is a dialectical process. Teachers cannot control the most important things that happen in class. They can only experience the process through humility. A teacher's work is judged by its long-term outcome, of which he or she can normally expect to know little or nothing. The teacher works largely in the dark (Metcalfe & Game 2006).

CONCLUSION

The Coleman Report, released in 1966, which looked at the achievement of 640, 000 students in grades one, three, six, nine, and twelve concluded the following: "Taking all these results together, one implication stands above all: that schools bring little to bear on a child's achievement that is independent of his background and general social context" (p. 235). This conclusion questioned the potential of schools and teachers to positively influence a student's achievement. While this conclusion holds some truth, additional research studies that followed the report provided evidence for a different conclusion. These studies demonstrated that effective schools can make a substantial difference in the achievement of students. A single most influential component of an effective school that emerged was the individual teacher.

A study by Nye, Konstantopoulos, and Hedges (1991) quantified the influence effective teachers have on student achievement. The study involved random assignment of students to classes controlled for factors such as the previous achievement of students, socioeconomic status, ethnicity, gender, class size, and whether or not an aide was present in class. This study answered the question of how much influence the individual classroom teacher has on student achievement. They summarized the results as follows: "These findings would suggest that the difference in achievement gains between having a 25 percentile teacher (a not so effective teacher) and a 75th percentile teacher (an effective teacher) is over one-third of a standard deviation (0.35) in reading and almost half a standard deviation (0.48) in mathematics. Similarly, the difference in achievement gains between having a 50th percentile teacher (an average teacher) and 90th percentile teacher (a very effective teacher) is about one-third of a standard deviation (0.33) in reading and somewhat smaller than half a standard deviation (0.46) in mathematics. . . ." (p. 253).

This study provides guidance on the nature of effective teaching. However, teachers know that there is no formula for effective teaching. Research has its own limitations. It will never be able to identify instructional strategies that work with every student in every class. The best that research can tell us is what strategies have a good chance to work in classrooms. Each individual teacher must determine how to work with students and what strategies work best (Marzano 2007).

Berliner (1986) concludes that effective teaching is a dynamic mixture of expertise in a vast array of instructional strategies, combined with a profound understanding of the individual students in class and their needs at particular points in time. Malcolm Gladwell, author of *Outliers: The Story of Success* and a former *Washington Post* reporter, compares teacher recruiting to the recruiting of quarterbacks in the National Football League. You never know how they will do until they get onto the field, under pressure, with split second decisions to make and everything at stake.

Metcalfe and Game (2006) comment that at the heart of education rests a tension between the desire for certainty and the need for trust and openness.

Parents want teaching to supply their children with decent values, skills, and knowledge. However, since the acquisition of these values, skills, and knowledge is based on learning, education is orientated to openness. Many debates in education are beyond resolution because they are based, without acknowledgement, on this existential dilemma. There is no way to bring stability to a system that needs openness.

Competent teaching means the ability to manage this tension between the desire for certainty and the need for openness. If policy makers truly value education, they need to develop this maturity of attitude—they need to realize that their demands and the policies they create may actually reduce educational opportunities by interfering with the direct relation between teachers and students. As Metcalfe and Game (2006) say, it is only when the awesome responsibility of teaching is recognized that teachers will be given the respect and the trust they need to get on with their life-changing work.

Chapter Two

Why Me?

Robert Frost writes, "I am not a teacher, I am an awakener." Why are people attracted to teaching? There must be some kind of social philosophy behind the decision to teach. Those engaged in teaching externalize this philosophy. William Ayers (1993) writes, "People are called to teaching because they love children and youth or because they love being with them, watching them open up and grow and become more able, more competent, more powerful in the world. They love what happens to themselves when they are with children, the ways in which they become their best selves" (p. 8).

Teaching differs in character from any other profession, and like anything else it is not for everyone. Children enter school with a lot of excitement. They are like question marks. Unfortunately, they often exist as a period, said Neil Postman, the late Paulette Goddard Chair of Media Ecology at New York University and chair of the Department of Culture and Communication.

I will always remember my fourth-grade teacher who was never satisfied with what I did. I did extremely well in fourth grade and yet he wanted more. Thinking back, I now understand what he tried to do and I will eternally remain grateful to this gentleman, because he taught me in his own way that nothing was out of my reach. We all can think of a teacher who dramatically influenced our lives.

In the narratives that follow, Barbara speaks about her sixth-grade teacher who tried to crush her dream of becoming a teacher. Resilient and determined, she went on to become an award winning math teacher. Elena introduces master teacher, Ms. Greenberg, her kindergarten teacher who exemplified caring and making each and every child feel special. Jackquelynn remembers Ms. Englander, who let her discover the world of inquiry, and Ms. Wolfson, who nurtured an appreciation of literature and creative

10

writing. Ursula's fifth-grade history and literature teacher, Frau Schweitzer, inspired her to become a teacher. Ursula, Elena, Jackquelynn, and Barbara write about their lives and reach beyond the romantic and surface reasons people give for becoming teachers.

BARBARA

Becoming a teacher was my goal since I was in sixth grade. I was born to Italian American parents. My father was a construction worker and my mother was a dressmaker. My dad never finished high school and my mom went to a vocational high school. They instilled in me an excellent work ethic. They wanted me to get a good education so I could contribute to better the society in which we lived. Even though my parents were not highly educated, we always had books, magazines, and newspapers in our apartment.

My father was taken out of high school to go to work at fifteen years of age. His father would not allow him to read, and threw out his books! Therefore, my dad became a self-educated man. Even though we grew up without a car, we went all over New York City—to museums, the theater, the beach, and the library!

Ever since I was able to read, my dad would always tell me that he wanted me to work with my head not my hands. His dream was to see me go to college. I had decided to become a teacher because I felt it would be an interesting and exciting profession.

The thought of working with children and seeing them develop and grow was a fascinating and inspirational idea.

However, my sixth-grade teacher crushed my dreams. During a parent-teacher meeting, my teacher told my parents I was not a good student and that she was taking me out of the top class. I was the only student to be taken out of the accelerated class that year. I was devastated by this and became disillusioned about what my life would become. I remember crying most of the summer and dreading going back to school in the fall. My parents encouraged me to work harder and never give up. After this horrible experience, I vowed that not only would I never give up my dream, but that when I became a teacher I would encourage and nurture my students to develop their abilities.

A teacher's focus should be on helping children feel comfortable in their learning environment, not fearful or stupid. Therefore, my philosophy was to be compassionate in my teaching methods while also remembering that my students would need to develop basic skills and acquire knowledge in order to become independent, confident, and competent in their lives.

ELENA

Well, there was never a doubt in my mind that I was going to be a kinder-garten teacher. Actually there was, but that was before I walked into Ms. Greenberg's kindergarten class when I had just turned five years old. So, for five years, I was unsure of my life's choice.

The first day was not as stellar as might be expected though. I had spent my first five years at home with my mother, while my sister and brother, five and four years older than me, respectively, were at school, and my father, sweet man that he was, was at work as a New York City sanitation worker. At home, there had probably been all the build up and celebration about the impending first day of school. The school was familiar to me. It was around the corner from our house. It was a classic NYC public school in blue-collar Cypress Hills, Brooklyn, all brick and high windowed, built in 1888 (as the stone work on the tall facade clearly announced), PS 65. I had been there many times, tagging along as my mother did Parent Teacher Association (PTA) activities. The T was still in the PTA way back then in 1953.

So off I went in my little, brand new Buster Brown school shoes and plaid dress, new haircut, and little satchel school bag—and then it dawned on me. Mommy was not going to come into the room with me! I was okay for about one second and then the tears came. So, immediately a deal was struck amongst us, Mommy, Ms. Greenberg, and me. Mommy would wait outside the door and watch through the small door window.

Ms. Greenberg expertly and lovingly took my hand and engaged me in the activities. She was only there for me or so I thought at the time. I was clueless to the fact that there were at least twenty-five other five-year-olds who were also suffering anxiety and were also being comforted by the only grown-up in the room.

Somehow, I found my way to a large table with about five other girls. There were table activities and games. Little did I know that these five girls would be my friends all the way through high school and beyond, Annette, Joanne, Vivian, Dorothy, and Carol. We were playing and laughing and then the little pang of angst began to grow, "Mommy. Oh, it's okay, she's at the door."

The morning went on and at snack time, I had to throw away my first container of school milk in the basket by the door. I thought I would wave to Mommy while I was doing my first kindergarten job. So I looked and stood on tippy-toe to peak out of the window in the door. No Mommy. Just as the tears were about to burst forth again, there was Ms. Greenberg's comforting hand to tell me that it was almost time to go home, that it was a half-day program and that Mommy was waiting at the pick-up area with the other grown-ups. And it was so. I bounded out at dismissal, and as my mother reported, "I picked her up, and she was a different person."

So, why me? How did Ms. Greenberg do that, be in the right place at the right time for a little girl; how did I wind up at just the right table? Vivian did not speak English, she chattered to us in Greek. How did we all get comforted and entertained and introduced to the culture of kindergarten, and wanted to go back the next day? Well, that's what I wanted to learn how to do for others.

That's the touchy feely side of the story. But what about the educator in me? Elementary, junior, high school, all at Brooklyn public schools, it was a classic and rich education. While trying to be a biology major, I always had that niggling feeling of wanting to become a kindergarten teacher. Finally, in my junior year of college, I had to commit. Early childhood education would be my major at my small New Jersey University.

Little did I know that I had fallen into a gem of a progressive education program. Little did I know that Ms. Greenburg had been in the vanguard of the progressive education movement. Finally, I had names for my memories. Hands-on activities, meeting times, nurture the individual, talk to the children, make each one feel special, process not product, I do and I understand, be kind to each other, experiment with materials, learning centers, cooperation, patience—the list of memories and sound pedagogic practice were coming together. I learned that I had been a part of an education theory since I was five years old. I had come full circle and was ready to change the world. And that I tried to do, one child at a time, for the next thirty-five years.

JACKQUELYNN

My earliest memories of school in the Bronx are of days filled with quiet wonder. I clearly remember sitting in a first-grade classroom where the teacher kept calling the attendance, but never my name. Finally, she figured out that I was sitting in the wrong classroom. I was quickly spirited off to Mrs. MacLaughlin where I remained for two years, first and second grade. P.S. 99 was a clean, modern school, about a block and a half away from my apartment. My mother could watch me cross the street and walk the long block to Stebbins Avenue from the window.

Generally, elementary school was uneventful. I sat quietly, learning my lessons, contented, until I got to third grade. I had a miserable teacher and spent my third-grade days in fear. I can never remember her smiling. It seemed as if she took all of her problems out on the class. Finally, I made it to fourth grade and a whole new wondrous world opened up in Mrs. Englander's class.

My fifth grade was spent with a woman whose homeroom was the library. Mrs. Borgstadt was just plain mean to children. I learned in her class firsthand about racial intolerance, from her comments about New York City's influx of Puerto Ricans. She used homework as a punishment. She was the only teacher, in my twelve-year history of public school that my mother actually confronted and questioned. She instilled a "fear of math" in me and did not allow questions in her class.

As Mrs. Englander had promised when we left her in fourth grade, she would see us in sixth grade and "undo all the damage done to us in fifth grade." She promised us that our last year at P.S.99 would be wonderful and it was! I remember Mrs. Englander was a war bride from Britain, tall, boney thin, smelled good, and wore fabulous clothes. I always blame her for introducing me to big earrings and fur. She was never without either. She had the patience of Job and opened the world of inquiry to us through countless hands-on projects.

I spent two years, grade four and grade six, in her nurturing hands. I think it was this woman that single-handedly planted the "seed of teaching" in my soul. Mrs. Englander possessed what I might now call the magic potion for teaching: personality, sensitivity, discipline, intelligence, communication skills, and most important, a love for children and teaching.

As I moved on to Junior High School 40, Bronx, it was a mixture of adolescent confusion, but the one thing that remained constant was my love of school. I ran to Mr. Levine's English classes with eager excitement, became the weather girl for Dr. Wright's science class, and began six years of violin lessons (very mediocre) with the school orchestra. As I moved to the Gothic building of Morris High School, still in the Bronx, for my final years, I discovered literature and a love of creative writing with Mr. Wolfson.

I learned stenography, taught by the quiet and very businesslike Mr. Zonano. On my own, I devoured historical novels. And then, suddenly, it was all over. I remember dissolving into tears at the end of the graduation ceremony. I had spent twelve wonderful, nurturing years in the school community. Friends were moving in other directions, college, work, marriage. What was to become of me?

While I was an above average student and counselors had advised I continue on to college, the financial situation at home did not make this a viable choice at the moment. So I entered the workforce, the Department of Welfare, where another kind of education began to take place. Previously extremely shy, I began to emerge from a kind of cocoon, making new adult friends. One of my coworkers wondered aloud why I was not in college and, as good friends do, pushed me towards that end. I found I could attend evening classes at Bernard Baruch College, New York. I did this for many years, starting, completing a term or two, then moving to many other schools. It seemed I was unfocused, could not decide on a major and I eventually dropped out. It would be many years before I entered school again.

However, life has many turns. As an administrative assistant for a foundation that offered educational incentives for employees, I first enrolled in Long Island University, New York where I obtained a paralegal certificate. Later, I enrolled at New York University (NYU), where the continuing education division provided ample counseling and guidance. Somehow, I was able to move effortlessly through their AA and BA programs. While attending NYU full-time and starting my own home business, I managed to graduate with a BA in international studies. However, I found moving into this field without a foreign language difficult.

Around the same time, a little girl in New York City named Lisa Steinberg was horribly tortured in the hands of her guardians and consequentially died in 1984. As all of NYC read about the incomprehensible abuse this six-year-old child had suffered, it nagged at me persistently that she had gone to school where bruises and her appearance were not questioned. In this country, it is our smallest citizens that get lost through a maze of paperwork and bureaucracy. There were interviews at her school with her teachers and all the people involved in her life. Internally, I felt that the school should have been more vigilant. I am sure on a personal level all of the people involved with Lisa Steinberg had played out their own scenarios. As a "village," we had all failed Lisa Steinberg and even today we continue to fail so many of our school-aged citizens. I think the seed of teaching began to take root. I wanted to be a vital part of the village.

During that same period, I visited the Friends School, in Manhattan, seeking job placement. It was the first time I had entered an elementary school since graduating. There was something familiar, but I could not put my finger on it. I was told I could substitute or even become a full-time teacher in the public or parochial school systems. I decided to spend a day at another Friends elementary school in Brooklyn, this time to observe through the eyes of a potential teacher. From the moment I stepped into the classroom, I realized that, finally, after many years of wandering, I had come home.

URSULA

After finishing high school in Heilbronn, Germany, at the age of seventeen, I had come up with a list of only the things I did not want to do. Since I had to do something, I signed up to work in an orphanage for a year. My work there included helping out in the kitchen and in the laundry room, but I spent most of my time with the children. It was a difficult year at the orphanage. The hours were long and I never had enough sleep or time for myself. I was working with children barely younger than me. Most of the children had come from troubled families and needed a lot of attention and support.

During that year, I applied to a two-year college in Stuttgart, Germany, to become a nursery school teacher. I looked forward to being back in school and living in Stuttgart, the capital and cultural center of the state of Baden Wuerttemberg. At the orphanage, it had been quite a challenge being the adult in charge of young children. I appreciated being back in the classroom as a college student. But working in the orphanage had also awakened in me a love for children and compassion for the less fortunate amongst them.

Nursery school teaching seemed like a good place for me to start. My own experience in nursery school had not been a very positive one. On my very first day there, I ran away. It was not that I missed my family; I just did not like the teacher. She was so very stern and unapproachable. Also, there were far too many children for me to feel comfortable. There were at least eighty. And there were definitely too many rules! The teacher had not even noticed that I had run away. Luckily, a neighbor found me on a street corner and took me back home. If only I could have been in Sister Mathilde's classroom next door! She smiled a lot and she talked to me even though I was not in her class. But I had to go back to school the next day. However, my mother made a deal with me and my sister. We would go to school in the morning and stay home in the afternoon to play as we pleased.

It was not until fifth grade that I had a teacher that I really liked and admired. Frau Schweitzer was a wonderful teacher and an amazing person. She was in her early fifties and had a husband and three children. At that time, women teachers usually were single or widowed. Even though she was a bit chubby and not very athletic, she took us on hiking trips and showed us how to ice skate in the winter. When I had to be hospitalized that year, she visited me and brought me letters from all of my classmates. Frau Schweitzer taught us history and literature. I will always remember her lessons about the great Greek myths. We sat at the edge of our seats, holding on to our desks for dear life, enthralled by Odysseus's voyage.

Frau Schweitzer had been a teacher in Stuttgart during World War II and had spent many hours in bomb shelters with her students. In those dark and scary places, she sat with her students, retelling Homer's *Odyssey* and *Iliad*. "When I grow up," I thought, "I want to be like Frau Schweitzer, intelligent, knowledgeable, kind and competent."

In seventh grade, I had yet another outstanding teacher in math. Herr Braun always started his lessons with a question, yet he did not expect an immediate answer. Instead, he wanted us to explore a variety of possible solutions, coaching us along the way. Little did I know that I was getting my first taste of progressive education.

Math with Herr Braun became my favorite subject. On the other hand, English, one of my foreign language requirements, was an academic stumbling block and a nightmare for me. My parents, even though they couldn't really afford it, hired a private tutor to help me. I was so ashamed of my poor performance and I felt guilty for the financial burden I caused my family. Still, my performance barely improved. Unfortunately, I had an English teacher who had no patience with struggling students like me. She mainly ignored us. She would not waste her time. She, gleefully, handed us our failing grades.

Reflecting on my own school experiences, I wanted to become a friendly, kind, and caring teacher like Sister Mathilde. I also wanted to make learning interesting and exciting like Herr Braun and Frau Schweitzer. I wanted to create a classroom atmosphere where it was safe to ask questions and also safe to make mistakes. I aspired to do everything in my power to help the students in my class become knowledgeable and competent adults.

After I finished college in Stuttgart in 1963, my teaching career took me to the United States and back to Germany. In 1968, ultimately, I was back in New York. I came to New York to join the father of my eighteen-month-old son. He was studying at Queens College and had rented a small apartment for us on West 109th Street. This is how I ended up on the Upper West Side.

For the first few months, I stayed at home with our son but I was not happy. I felt isolated and bored. Also, we desperately needed to supplement my husband's meager academic stipends. I joined a parent co-op, The Children's Free School on Morningside Drive, for our son's day care needs, and started looking for a part-time job. A friend arranged an interview for me for an office job downtown. I thought that I really wanted the job. I was eager to get out of the house and to earn some money. But, during my job interview, all I talked about was how much I liked teaching. The interviewer was very kind. He said, "I can offer you the job but I don't think you want it. Go back to teaching."

With only my German credentials, I could not find a teaching position. However, I was able to substitute in city-funded day care centers. Within a few months, I was offered a position as a teacher's aide in one of the centers where I had been substituting. Shortly afterward, I went back to college. After receiving a BA from Antioch College and an MS from Bank Street College of Education, I became a licensed New York City public school teacher.

As I entered "the system," I promised myself to be an excellent teacher but not to get too involved in school politics. I had seen too many wonderful teachers burned, trying to change the system. Instead, I was going to make a difference in the lives of the children in my class, one child at a time, one family at a time, and one day at a time. That's what I knew how to do best.

Ms. Greenberg, Ms. Englander, Ms. Wolfson, Frau Schweitzer, and Barbara's sixth-grade teacher, wherever they might be today, do not know that they awakened a passion in the children they taught. They were the awakeners Robert Frost talked about. They allowed their students to dream and think of the possibilities ahead even though many children live in exile from their dreams. They motivated their students to affirm their dreams and realize their potential. They hoped for a better future for their students. Thankfully, for Barbara, Elena, Jackquelynn, and Ursula, teaching became their life's mission and gift to the next generation.

Chapter Three

My First Year Teaching

All first-year teachers share a common experience that can be both humbling and rewarding. Teaching for the first time is often a baptism by fire. The neophyte teacher enters uncharted, unpredictable, and ever changing territories. No book or course will ever prepare a new teacher for that first day. The idea is to learn by doing, building the plane in flight. Even for a veteran teacher, good teaching remains a mystery. There is no single description of a good teacher.

Kane (1991) writes, "The challenges and difficulties of teaching may also be the factors that make it appealing, particularly to young men and women who are eager to make a difference in the lives of others and to test their own abilities. In almost any other kind of work open to recent college graduates, new employees are given limited duties the first year on the job. It takes months, sometimes years, before the neophytes are considered sufficiently seasoned to handle increased responsibility or to make the kind of independent decisions that teachers must make the first day on the job. Indeed, few other jobs offer the immediate challenges, the magnitude of responsibility, or the potential for intrinsic satisfaction and learning that teaching in an elementary school or secondary school affords from the first day of employment" (p. 1).

Elena, Jackquelynn, and Ursula talked about "many first years" of teaching. Elena talked about being full of bravado on the outside, but adrift and confused on the inside. Jackquelynn writes, "My first year I was a teacher! I was a student! I learned eagerly with my students. My firsts were hard, demanding, joyful, sad, hurtful, enthusiastic, creative, and very emotional." Ursula pointed out that she almost gave it up but for the help of her next door colleague. Her colleague not only helped her discipline her students but also shared teaching ideas and supported her in the community, assuring the parents that the new teacher was doing fine.

19

If the first year teaching is baptism by fire as the cliché holds, Barbara was an exception. What is a rule without exception? Her first year teaching experience was a love story in her own words. She was fortunate to have completed her student teaching in the school where she was appointed. She was familiar with the building. She had a sense of the dress code and, more importantly, she knew many of the school staff members. Unlike many other teachers, her familiarity with the school made her first year a positive experience. She writes, "The best part of my first year was that I actually felt like a teacher."

Here is Barbara in her own words.

BARBARA

September 1965 was the beginning of a love story for me! It was the start of my career as a teacher at P.S. 145. Who knew I would stay there for thirty-two years! My first class of thirty-five students was a daunting experience. In front of me, fourth graders with eager eyes, new clothes, new sneakers, broad smiles, and book bags that were bigger than them—my start as a teacher began.

I was fortunate to have done my student teaching at P.S. 145, so the administration, staff, and some of the students were familiar to me. I also knew the different parts of the building. This enabled me to locate the gym, cafeteria, library, bathrooms, and teachers' room. This may sound silly, but when you are first starting in a new school, it is important to know where you are going!

My students were mainly Hispanic and African-American. And, believe it or not, one of them, Maryann, became our school secretary many years later at P.S. 145! I remember only one student who was very difficult. Charles was a very angry and frustrated little boy. He banged on the desk, called out constantly and did no work. He was only one out of a class of thirty-five. I remember that I had to keep a behavioral log and notify his mother daily. I had to speak to the guidance counselor on a weekly basis. I had full support from the administration. Teaching was so different then. I even made house calls with the social worker. Finally, in March, Charles got suspended because he punched a pregnant teacher in the stomach!

I remember that besides teaching all the subjects, reading, math, science, English, gym, social studies, we were responsible for two plays a year, weekly assemblies, attendance programs, and a class trip for fourth grade. And, heaven forbid, should you need to go to the bathroom. We had no preps then.

I also had to write a plan book. It was collected each week by the assistant principal and it was returned with comments, suggestions, and criticisms! We also had many meetings each week and faculty meetings once a month. The assistant principal frequently observed me, and the principal did so twice a year. They observed the lesson and provided constructive feedback.

I decorated the hallway bulletin board with the students' work. This was a creative, pedagogical, and appropriate outlet for my students. I remember the wonderful support I received from my colleagues including eleven new teachers the year I started. We were colleagues and also became friends.

The tone of the school was very upbeat and pleasant. When the principal walked into a classroom, the students and the teacher greeted him with respect. He would spend a few minutes talking to class each day. Not only did the principal take time to visit the class but he also knew what was happening throughout the school.

The ability to instruct my students in the fourth year curriculum program and not be bogged down with "nonsense" made my first year a great experience. The best part of my first year was that I actually felt like a teacher.

Ellen Moir (2004), director of teacher education at the University of California in Santa Cruz, and director of the New Teacher Center at UCSC and the Santa Cruz New Teacher Project, distinguishes five stages a new teacher goes through in his or her first year. However, the teacher does not experience them linearly. They include the anticipation stage, the survival stage, the disillusionment stage, the rejuvenation stage, and the reflection stage.

The anticipation stage involves an idealistic view of the teaching profession. This phase begins during student teaching, when one visualizes what it is like to be a teacher. The soon-to-be teachers romanticize their role and their position and, more importantly, how they are going to make a difference in the lives of children at a time when some of them may not even have a clue about the student population they are going to work with.

The survival stage is a time when the new teachers confront a variety of problems and situations they did not anticipate. Teaching is often unpredictable. The realization that it is not a nine-to-five job sets in. Lessons have to be prepared. Curriculum must be developed. There is little time to stop and reflect on their day to day experience. This is the stage when most new teachers struggle to keep their heads above water.

The disillusionment stage is a disenchantment phase when the new teachers realize that things are not going as smoothly as they want, and low morale sets in. They question their commitment as well as their competence. They express self-doubt, experience low self-esteem. Moir (2004) remarks that getting through this phase may be the toughest challenge a teacher faces.

The rejuvenation stage shapes a teacher's attitude informed by lessons learned in the process. The teacher hopefully develops a better understanding of the school system, an acceptance of realities of teaching, and a sense of accomplishment. Learning from their experience, teachers begin to develop coping strategies to help them address problems that they encounter in the second part of the year. Armed with new coping strategies, they feel confident and experience a sense of relief that they made it through.

The reflection stage offers an opportunity to reflect on successes and failures. The teachers reflect on the various changes they initiated as they moved along. They decide what worked and what did not. They draw lessons from the past to prepare for the future.

Moir's framework is a useful tool to make sense out of the first year teaching experience. However, each teacher experiences that first year in unique ways. Certainly the anticipation stage is common to all teachers. Before getting into a job, we imagine ourselves in the job. This is a powerful way to materialize our expectations. The survival stage represents an adaptation to one's new environment. The disillusionment stage is a phase when one wonders about the choice made. Rejuvenation and reflection go together. Whenever teachers reflect on what they are doing in a classroom, they are giving themselves the opportunity to rejuvenate their thoughts and try new strategies.

Elena, Jackquelynn, and Ursula experienced various aspects of these phases.

ELENA

Like most things in my life, the beginning of my teaching career was strange. My first year of classroom teaching was really my third year of teaching. When we think about our first year of teaching, it is usually about being full of bravado on the outside, but being adrift and confused on the inside. From the stories I have heard from others, the first year is often plagued with non-supportive administration, a paucity of supplies, and confusing bureaucracy.

In December 1968, after spending months traveling in Spain (on five dollars a day) following my graduation in June, I finally decided it was time to get real with employment. I was lucky to be living with my supportive parents, and the necessity of a salary was not yet knocking on my door. At twenty years old, independence and a car, however, were of interest. Unbeknownst to me, and again one of the mysteries and happenstances of my life, I had succeeded in avoiding the major, divisive, and pivotal NYC teachers' strike that occurred in the fall of 1968. I dabbled in being a substitute in various schools in upper Manhattan and the Bronx, and as fate would have it, I landed at P.S. 123 in Harlem just in time for the days before the Christmas vacation. Lots of teachers were out on the days before Christmas. Christmas must have been on a Thursday that year, so with Wednesday off for Christmas Eve, many teachers helped themselves to Monday and Tuesday to have an extended two-week vacation.

The administration was thrilled to have somebody, actually anybody, available for those two days.

Those days stretched into eighteen years. Hey, you never know! I substituted at P.S. 123 all through January, and when the new term started on February 1, I was offered a position. In a meeting of less than five minutes, the principal, who was a nice guy in a menschy kind of NYC way, asked me, just like this, "So, Elena, do you want to be a cluster teacher or an Open Corridor teacher?" Little did I know that this would be one of the most important decisions of my life (another was being forced by my union chapter chair, Lenny Lowy, another mensch, to sit down with him and fill out and sign my pension enrollment papers when I was twenty-two and I really only wanted to party).

I definitely did know that I did not want to be a cluster teacher. A cluster or prep teacher was one who went to many classes during the day and gave teachers their breaks. This was a position that had just been created after the contentious strike of 1968. It was an unformed concept. Basically, it was babysitting for forty-five minutes classes of kids whom I didn't know, with no curriculum. Somehow I knew it was not for me. So I said, "Okay, I will be the Open Corridor teacher."

He briefly explained that it was a new program from the City College of New York (CCNY) with Professor Lillian Weber. P.S. 123 had been chosen to pilot the program, not because of its great commitment to progressive education but because of its proximity to CCNY, down the steep block from academia to the Harlem valley.

I would set up and supervise hands-on activities in a corridor adjacent to five classrooms of teachers who were committed to trying this new progressive style of teaching. The children flowed in and out of the classrooms throughout the day, participating in rich and fun hands-on and interactive activities. There have been books written on this program and it would be too much to include them here. An excellent article presenting an overview of the open classroom movement is available in *Education Next: A Journal of Opinion and Research* (http://www.hoover.org/publications/ednext/3288371.html).

Well, it was a love fest. There were thousands of dollars worth of new materials, Cuisenaire rods, pattern blocks, markers, reams of various types of paper, water and sand tables, and Unifix, to name a few. These were all cutting-edge materials coming out of the English Infant School progressive education project which Lillian Weber studied and was introducing to the educators of the United States. "I do, I understand" was the mantra of the program.

This happily went on until June 1970, when District 5 of the NYC Board of Education, P.S. 123's district, decided that this hands-on program was not for their children. District 5 bosses pontificated that their children needed structure and old-fashioned teaching and homework. So, in a nutshell, Lillian Weber and The Open Classroom went on to more welcoming green pastures in District 3 where they flourished at schools like P.S. 84, P.S. 87, and P.S. 75 for decades. District 5 did not flourish within The Open Classroom ideology, neither did I. I often have reflected on and wondered why I was not invited to go along and transfer to the new downtown school; nor did I ask to go along. I was a pedagogic casualty of a bigger project. If I had transferred, I would have certainly experienced a different journey.

So, I stayed at P.S. 123 and because of that I met my domestic partner and had three daughters. Interesting, how life turns out.

Inevitably, sixteen years later, I did transfer to District 3 and reunite with many of the teachers and staff developers who were colleagues of mine at CCNY in our Masters Program with Lillian Weber. We had all been on parallel journeys spreading the word of progressive education, working with one child at a time.

Back to my first year of teaching which was really my third year; The Open Classroom was no more, and the next September I was a second-grade teacher. Now, reality set in. The support system of my corridor teachers was gone. They were still in the building but scattered all around. The influx of fabulous materials had ended. The support of professors was elsewhere. Fortunately, I was already established in the school with a good reputation and a cadre of friends. In 1970, there were not many supplies. Staff development was nonexistent. The administration had changed from supportive to disruptive. The kids thought our principal was the lunchroom lady because that was the only time they saw her, yelling at them in the cafeteria. We had basal readers and math workbooks.

Upon reflection, I now recognize that this is where I learned to close my door, smile and nod at administrators, and continue my progressive style of teaching. Basal readers and math workbooks became supplementary to a hands-on, interactive, and integrated curriculum. I was making it up as we went along. Conditions were horrible, lots and lots of roaches, smelly bathrooms and stairwells. There were announcements over the public announcement system from the principal to remind us to keep the boys from participating in making more "effluvial odors from the radiators in the bathrooms," more simply put, "get them to stop urinating on the heaters!"

Yikes! I was twenty-two years old. I loved my job and I loved the kids and the kids loved me and by extrapolation, most of the parents loved and respected me. The families were trying to survive and get a good education for their kids. We were surrounded by poverty, drugs, and burned out hulks of buildings, six-story walk-up tenements, and towering housing projects. There were little to no services. This was years before we had School Based Support Teams of guidance counselors, psychologists, social workers, family workers, and advocates. The classroom teachers wore all of these hats. Common sense ruled, that is, if you had any. The older teachers and their methods were clashing with the younger, more liberal and progressive ones. Corporal punishment was tolerated by administrators and most parents. We were the first to employ "don't ask, don't tell."

Yet, I really did go to work happily every day. I cannot remember much of the daily routines and methods. The neighborhood folks were kind to me. They watched my car, a little blue VW convertible Karman Ghia. I was never harassed. I felt safe and protected in the neighborhood. Inside the school, there certainly was a lot of frustration and anger about administrative blunders and inane directives, about out-of-control children, and families and ineffective teachers who burdened the rest of us.

Yes, I really do believe that first year in the classroom was the beginning of my strategy of my own little one room schoolhouse. It was just me and the kids.

JACKQUELYNN

I could say I had many "first" years of teaching. The firsts were my first year of teaching at St. Joseph's, the first year at the Wadleigh School for Writing and Publishing, and finally, my first year as an early childhood teacher at P.S. 145.

My master's program at Fordham University consisted of teaching full-time at St. Joseph's Parochial School, attending evening classes, and working with a mentor who monitored my teaching twice weekly.

After an initial interview at Fordham, Sister Grace chose me and another teacher, Carrie Lewis (with whom I have shared a wonderful professional and personal relationship since our first meeting) to head her third-grade class. The class consisted of thirty-five students divided into two adjacent classrooms. Science and social studies were taught to both groups, with me teaching the latter. Together, we planned activities, trips, and teaching strategies, and bounced ideas off each other. It was, perhaps one of my best working relationships in education. It was extremely meaningful to have the support of fellow teachers.

I entered a classroom with eighteen eight- and nine-year-olds, who beamed with anticipation. The parents handed them over to me with mixed emotions of trust and trepidation. As for me, my heart beat so fast and hard that I thought it was going to explode. I think it was the normal fear of beginning a new career in midlife. Everything seemed to be thrown at me at once, administrative duties, lesson plans, curriculum, school rules and regulations, assessment of students, classroom management, and writing term papers as I continued to work on my masters in education.

I remember that time as being stressful as I tried to cope with it all. Whenever my fellow teachers and I met for our graduate classes, I realized that I was managing far better than most of the other teachers. Friction had developed with the pairings in other schools, and I learned early on that petty professional jealousy could be detrimental within the school environs. The school community is not unlike other workplaces. The human element will always surface: jealousy, competitiveness, insecurities, etc. These emotions can often hinder the primary efforts for being in a school.

In my first year, I was the teacher! I was also the student! I learned as eagerly as my students. I learned about mealworms and discovered Turkish Delight as we all traveled through *The Lion, the Witch and the Wardrobe*. On a snowy day, we imagined and painted "sunflakes," inspired by the poem. I learned to see New York City through the eyes of third graders as we traveled through museums, parks, and zoos.

I was amazed at how children had evolved since I had been a child. Children seemed to be more outspoken in class and to be greater risk takers than I remembered as a child. And they talked constantly. As my year at St. Josephs ended I was overcome with emotion. I had given a part of my heart to eighteen souls.

Next, I formally entered the NYC Board of Education equipped with my master's, as the sixth-grade Language Arts Teacher (a permanent sub-position). This was another first! Middle school was a brand new ballgame. Raging hormones, anger, frustration, and below-average skills permeated the halls. The School for Writing and Publishing was in its first year and housed in P.S. 113 until the renovations were completed at Wadleigh School. It was this year that I witnessed students who had gone through a school system where the educational system and society had failed them. I looked at record cards where attendance records were spotty at best: poor attendance, by child and parent, frequent moves from one school to another, repeating of grades, and lack of motivation occurred every day. However, the opening of the School for Writing and Publishing offered a unique opportunity to intervene in what was surely an ever-increasing routine of destruction and failure.

The School was one of the new mini-schools being formed across New York City. Each had its own unique program headed by a different director. Susan W., with a group of teachers from Wadleigh, had put together this unique program that focused on the "whole child," with emphasis on writing. Students applied to this middle school and each of them was interviewed. They were enthusiastic to participate in my new program. The staff was small: two language art teachers, one math specialist, one social studies teacher, one science teacher, and two generalists. The staff also included a social worker, one very popular but troublesome paraprofessional, one administrative assistant, and an office worker. This small and intimate staff created an odd mixture. Most of the staff had worked together in the previous school. I, along with two others, joined the school in 1991.

The school offered Prep for Prep, a program preparing students to test into elite preparatory boarding schools in the eighth grade. This program was run by a no-nonsense gentleman, Eduardo P., who not only taught math, but offered training in the social graces that would be expected of them at prep schools.

We traveled extensively, as a whole school. To my amazement, so many students had never been south of 113th Street. In fact, from our location at West 113th Street and Lenox Avenue, just across from Mt. Morris Park, many students had never crossed the park to Broadway. These students seemed to have lived in a self-imposed vacuum.

Because the school was so small, occupying only half of the third floor, it fostered quite an intimate atmosphere. It seemed as if everyone was involved in everyone else's business. This was something I was not accustomed to, coming from the outside business world. I soon became uncomfortable with this. The troublesome paraprofessional was a loudmouth and a bully. That first year, I seemed to be her target. In an open meeting, she actually accused me of not being "black enough" for the students, and I should go back to the East side where I probably hung out on the weekends. I had never been subjected to such hostility on a job. It was one of my darkest moments in education.

But one of my brightest moments occurred at the establishment of the after-school book club. I started this club, which greatly increased the number of books written, published, and handmade by the students. In this after-school club, I was able to form more intimate relations with students who were eager to share their own stories in writing. This informal, relaxed atmosphere yielded a rich series of self-published books.

As I began my second year at the School for Writing and Publishing, the results of the Common Branch and Early Childhood exams were published. I am thankful for a phone call that Susan put in to District 3 when I was about to be appointed. She thought I deserved to be in a better school than P.S. 113. She asked that I be kept in District 3. Later, I went for an interview at P.S. 145 with Judy Budd and Myra Langford. I sat between these women feeling like l was buffered by two bookends. The interview was pleasant and effortless. Upon leaving the meeting, I stopped by the phone booth to make a call; Judy came running out to catch up with me, saying, "We'll take you!" I have often wondered what was said in the short time it took to make their selection. Whatever it was, whatever impression I might have made, I was grateful they had selected me.

Two weeks later, I was ensconced in Room 122, which was one room away from the principal's office. The first grade had filed a grievance for excess children and they were making up a new class. Thus began my third "first."

The classroom had formerly belonged to a teacher who had retired, and basic supplies should have been available. But, as the mice will play when the cat is away, the room was bare and had obviously been raided. My class included every problem child in all the overcrowded first-grade classes. I got some very difficult kids.

I struggled trying to figure out schedules, reading groups, and what to teach. Teaching manuals were thrust into my hand for reading, writing, arithmetic, handwriting, science, and social studies. There was no group planning like I had done with Carrie in third grade at St. Joseph's. I was responsible for everything. The first weeks were quite chaotic. On returning one lunch hour, I actually lost a student. Checking the attendance for the afternoon, I could not account for Louis. After panicking, I finally found Louis curled up asleep on the floor of the coat closet!

I learned lessons the hard way. Through these lessons, I developed class rules. One example that remained consistent was to allow only one child at a time at the water fountain. This came about when a child cut the cord to the aquarium. With students clustered at the fountain, it blocked my view of the electrical system. Learning to develop a "third eye" is essential in teaching.

During my first year at P.S. 145, I had the good fortune to have Laura Diaz assigned to me, the best paraprofessional I would ever work with. She came to me in midterm. Laura was my left hand, and instinctively knew where in the classroom she was needed. I have never had the opportunity to repeat that experience. The value of having an extra, competent, and intelligent hand in teaching is a scarcity.

My first experiences were difficult, demanding, joyful, sad, hurtful, enthusiastic, creative, and emotional.

URSULA

During my teaching career, I had various first years. There was my first year as a teacher in the United States, my first year in the New York City public school system, and my first year at P.S. 145.

My very first year of teaching was in a kindergarten in Germany. The word "kindergarten" was coined by Froebel. The literal translation is "garden of children." A traditionally Froebel kindergarten is a self-directed preschool. A kindergarten usually consists of a few classrooms and a large outdoor play area. Typically, three- to six-year-old preschool children work together in the same classroom. It is different from the American Kindergarten, which takes place in an elementary school and only refers to the year before first grade.

I was twenty-one and fresh out of college. Finally, I was an adult, or so I thought. I had my college degree and a real job. Nevertheless, for economic reasons, I decided to move back home with my parents and ended up writing lesson plans on my old childhood desk. There were numerous benefits to living back home. Besides the low rent, there was my mom's good cooking and I found an audience and sounding board for my daily school stories and adventures at our dinner table.

I was very excited to have my own classroom. As happens to so many young and new teachers, I was on a mission to improve and enrich the lives of my charges. I wanted the children to have fun in school and I wanted them to be free to express themselves. At that time, most of the schools in my community had an authoritarian approach to teaching. Old-fashioned punishments, like spanking or having a child sit in a corner, were still practiced.

Just before my graduation from college in Stuttgart, my teachers gave us their final advice. Knowing how excited we were and how ready we were to take on the old kindergarten establishment, they cautioned us to be patient. They counseled us to first become familiar with our schools and their communities before initiating any big changes. This, indeed, was very good advice and I would like to pass it on to future school chancellors, school administrators, and teachers. Good and new ideas are great, but as the saying goes, "Don't throw the baby out with the bath water!" Also, before you can ask your school community to trust you, you have to earn their confidence.

So, on that first day of my brand new teaching career, I donned my teacher's apron and became "Tante Ursula." In the time-honored Froebel tradition, teachers in kindergarten were addressed as auntie.

From 8 a.m. to 9 a.m. my sixty-five kindergarteners arrived, one by one, and settled themselves into our "free play" period. All went smoothly. This was the children's favorite time of the day. At 9:45 a.m., it was time to clean up and get ready for our next activity. I had adhered to the typical kindergarten clean-up protocol starting with the five-minute warning, followed by the clean-up song. But I only achieved a small rate of compliance. What to do? So I began to clean up, one table at a time. I sang to myself making up words as I moved about, "It's time to put the beads away, all you little children . . . It's time to put the crayons away . . ." and on and on. Suddenly, little voices and little hands joined in and I sang and we sang and cleaned up until the last building blocks had been put away. From then on, singing became my mode of coping with difficult and joyous occasions in the classroom. There are songs for almost every circumstance, for riding on the train, for running through the park, "I'll chase you round the bushes . . ." by Woody Guthrie, for a dismissal in the pouring rain. If you can't think of a song, you just make it up. Little kids like to make up songs themselves and, besides, they don't know the difference between a made-up and a traditional nursery song yet. It is much better to sing than to shout or holler at the children. They can and will join you in the singing and whatever you are trying to accomplish then becomes a shared effort. Even on my last day of teaching, I sang to my children as I dismissed them for the very last time.

It was on my second day that things got a little out of hand. We were nearing the end of clean-up time and I had quietly complimented myself on how well it was going. Just then, dear little Gabriela jumped on top of her table and began to dance. When I asked her to please come down and sit back in her chair, she just laughed and danced harder. By now, the whole class was watching and some of the children definitely considered following suit. And there, in the nick of time, Tante Elizabeth from next door materialized in our classroom. In no time, Gabriela was down from her table. To make certain there would not be another incident, she told Gabriela to come along for a visit to her classroom. Then, Tante Elizabeth turned to me, and making sure that everybody in the class could hear her, she said, "Any time anybody gives you trouble, Tante Ursula, you just send them right over." I don't know if I would have made it through those first weeks without her kind help.

After a few months of teaching, I had a terrible sore throat. Constant talking and singing, exposure to a barrage of germs from sniffling and coughing children, I was literally speechless. Immediately, I went to a nose and throat specialist for help. How could I teach without being able to talk? While I was sitting in the examining chair, my mouth wide open and with the doctor poking around in the back of my throat, I got a lecture and no sympathy at all. "You teachers," he said, "you talk too much, if you would only talk half as much, it would be much better for the students." I would have liked to defend myself but I was plainly in no position to do so. And of course he was right and I did remember his advice for the rest of my teaching career.

That year we had a beautiful autumn. I rode my bicycle to school every day. I rode along the Neckar River where I watched the barges going by, dreaming of the places of their destination, the Rhine River, Switzerland, Holland, France. I watched the leaves change color and the grapes ripen in the vineyards. The ride to and from school was a special time.

One day, I decided to take a detour and walk home with Gabriela and her sister Cindy. Gabriela still was often disagreeable in school. I considered myself a modern teacher who guided the children with kindness and explanations. Most of the time it worked, but not with Gabriela. This was a bit of a surprise, since her sister, just a year older than Gabriela, was no problem at all. Actually, I should not have been surprised. I myself was the second girl in my family and had sometimes been a troublemaker. But, one easily forgets.

After a few months of teaching, I still had not met the girls' mother or father. That was not unusual. Many of my students came to school by themselves. All the way to the girls' house, Gabriela trotted quietly alongside me as I walked my bike. She glanced at me now and then without saying a word while her sister and I chatted. Usually, it was Gabriela who did the talking. After a good ten minutes' walk, we reached our destination. In those days, many households did not have telephones, so it was not unusual or considered impolite for a visitor to show up unannounced. We rang their doorbell and their mother came out to greet us, with the girls' baby brother in her arms. She was a little surprised to see me as I awkwardly held on to my bicycle. I too was surprised when I saw her but tried not to show it. I had not expected this mother of three to be barely my own age. Before I could say a word, the mother started apologizing to me. She was sorry that I had to trouble myself and come all this way to see her. Yes, she had wanted to come and talk to me. She knew about Gabriela's poor behavior in school. Cindy had kept the family informed. Both she and her husband had been talking to Gabriela about it. She continued to confide that Gabriela was giving her a lot of trouble at home, too. She couldn't understand why. Gabriela was so much more difficult to raise than her older daughter Cindy. What should she do? Did I have any advice? I felt rather discomfited being asked for advice when I myself had come for help from the mother. I tried to imagine myself in her place, pots on the stove, a baby in her arms, and a husband on his way home from work. And then there were her two little girls back from school with the new teacher. She looked so vulnerable! Instead of complaining about the problems with Gabriela at school, I tried to reassure the mother. I promised to do my best to help Gabriela improve her behavior not only in school but also at home. We parted pleasantly. The girls waved and smiled as the mother rushed back inside. Gabriela and Cindy seemed to have enjoyed my visit.

From then on, at dismissal time, as I shook hands with each of my sixty-five students as our farewell ritual, I spent a little extra time with Gabriela. I would remind her not to give her mother a hard time. She would smile and nod. Gabriela and I had become a team, helping her mother.

During that first year of teaching, I experienced a great tragedy in one of my students' families. The mother of the student had committed suicide. I had met the mother, a beautiful young woman with two lovely children. In the morning, she often brought the little girl to school on her bicycle, and then, in the afternoon, picked her up with the baby brother in his pram. Her name was Ursula. We were *namens schwestern*, namesakes. There was a special stillness about her face that reminded me of old Dutch paintings. Even today, I can picture her. One day, instead of the mother, a neighbor came with the baby brother to pick up the little girl. The elderly woman explained to me that the mother had to be taken to the hospital in Weinsberg and that she had been there before. The hospital in Weinsberg was the psychiatric clinic for the area. A few days later, the father came to see me and he explained that the mother was suffering from schizophrenia. So sad! A few weeks later, the father came again, tears streaming down his face. He had come to tell me that the mother had taken her own life. "I don't blame them at the hospital," he said. "They couldn't watch her every minute." I was stunned and all I could do was to cry with the father. Nothing in my teacher training could have prepared me for all the realities of life.

At the end of the year I was ready to move on. I had saved enough money to buy a ticket to America. I have been saving up for buying transatlantic tickets ever since.

In this chapter, Barbara, Elena, Jackquelynn, and Ursula unveil their joys, struggles, and their fears. What stands out is their commitment to children and their untainted optimism repeatedly put to the test and emerging intact. They remained themselves, they loved their children and they loved teaching.

Chapter Four

What Worked for Me?

Teaching is unpredictable. Had it not been, each and every teacher would have the right formula to educate children and make them successful. Joseph McDonald (1992), a professor at New York University, writes that there is a conspiracy of certainty in teaching that promotes sanitized images of teaching. Teaching amounts to a complex task that must address the social, political, economic, and cultural realities of the students. A teacher must know his or her students and, more importantly, what they bring to school with them.

Besides knowing the students, teaching is an encounter with the self (Gibson 1998). It is learning and being mindful. Ellen Langer, a professor of psychology at Harvard University, talks about helping people realize that the world is full of interesting possibilities for learning. Quoted in *Parade* magazine, she says, "Too often, we teach people things like, 'there's a right way and a wrong way to do everything, regardless of the circumstances.' What we should be teaching them is how to think flexibly, to be mindful of all the different possibilities of every situation and not close themselves off from information that could help them." Learning is a meaning-making process that involves interpretation, analysis, reflection, and contemplation (Mezirow 1991).

Unfortunately, our policy makers' addiction to high-stakes testing blinds them from what teaching and learning are all about. Rather than children pursuing knowledge, knowledge is pursuing children. Ernest L. Boyer (1993), the renowned education expert and then President of the Carnegie Foundation for the Advancement of Teaching, wrote, "I know how idealistic it may sound, but it is my urgent hope that in the century ahead students in the nation's schools will be judged not by their performance on a single test, but by the quality of their lives. It is my hope that students in the classrooms of tomorrow will be encouraged to be creative, to conform and learn to cooperate rather than compete."

As a teacher, I always ask myself the following questions after each lesson: What did I teach; what did I learn; and what did the students learn. If I do not learn, why should I expect my students to learn? Dewey (1929) observed that uncertainty saves a place for novelty and genuine growth and change. Allowing uncertainty and doubt informs our relationships to practical problems. It is that sense of uncertainty and doubt that Barbara, Elena, Jackquelynn, and Ursula capture when talking about what worked for them.

BARBARA

Making Math Fun

In the early 1970s, before preparation periods were a part of a teacher's day, I was a fourth-grade teacher teaching thirty-five students without a break. With the advent of preparation periods, the need for cluster teachers developed. My friend, Sandra Sanders, developed a math cluster program in her school in the Bronx. We discussed the possibility of developing a similar math cluster in my school. I shared the idea with my principal who gladly approved it.

I began P.S. 145's first math cluster with a can of rulers combined with my imagination and a strong motivation. My goal was to make math exciting and fun. It was important to me to make the program worthwhile and not just a time filler so that teachers could have a break.

In order to make the math program different, I enrolled in a special Saturday program called the Madison Project, where a group of teachers developed an exciting program using math manipulatives, math tapes, math games, and other hands-on activities, to help students learn mathematics and enjoy the process as well. In those early days, the cluster program was perceived as an innovative and creative way of teaching mathematics.

Progressively, I collected mathematics materials to use in the classes I taught. Starting with just a can of rulers, I began to use math Cuisenaire rods, three-dimensional geometric solid figures, compasses, protractors, tangrams, money, graphing activities, liquid containers, etc.

I finally got a rolling cart to carry these materials to my classes. The students and teachers readily accepted this hands-on approach to teaching mathematics. We had math contests, math bulletin boards, a problem of the week later known as Math Mind Benders (my colleague, Frieda Offen, eventually developed it into a schoolwide program).

For several years, I roamed the halls of P.S. 145 with my math cart. Finally, the principal assigned me a room. Now, my math program really took off, as the Math Lab room became a reality. At first, the teachers brought their classes to my room so they could have their prep time. I set up the room in separate focus areas for the students. The room had a graph table, a number work table, a fraction table, and a measurement and geometry table. These areas were further supported by the presence of four computers in the back of the room. In addition, there was a math listening area with tapes on math numeration. The students came to math lab twice a week. One day they would have a lesson on a math topic their teacher selected and the other day the students would select a math table to work on.

Each student had a math folder to keep track of the activities he or she engaged in. This enabled me to make sure they rotated their activity each week.

Eventually, the math program became a major part of the school curriculum. A math coordinator, Janice Clark, headed the District 3 math programs. Each school was given $5,000 worth of materials to enhance their labs. At the monthly math meetings with Mrs. Clark, we developed a districtwide Math Lab Program. As I look back, I think I was ahead of my time. Finally, mathematics was recognized as an important part of the elementary school student's learning experience. In addition to this, we received federal funding for the program.

The monthly meetings were held at different schools each week so we could learn from each other and see different laboratory setups. We also had special meetings at book publishing locations such as McGraw-Hill, in Manhattan, and Cuisenaire, in New Rochelle. We received free materials at these publisher meetings to add to our programs.

My math lab experience came full circle when my students involved themselves in a citywide Math Olympics and won an award. My laboratory was also cited by a state math administrator as one of the best math labs in the state of New York.

Being Visible: My Year as Acting Assistant Principal

On September 7, 1998, I began a year as an acting assistant principal. Our assistant principal (AP) had retired and our principal was very ill. I was asked to occupy this position until a licensed AP could be hired.

Up until this point, my career in education had been both dynamic and varied. I had been a fourth-grade teacher, a math lab teacher, a staff developer, and a teacher trainer for student teachers, for many years. I served as the school treasurer and was the school's union delegate to the United Federation of Teachers (UFT). In addition, I also gave math workshops to parents and teachers on a regular basis. However, nothing, absolutely nothing, could compare with the experience of being in an administrative position.

I imagine the reader thinking that an AP's position consists of being an educational advisor, instructing teachers on the curriculum and teaching methods for their respective grade levels. The reader may also think that an AP has a nice office with all of the latest educational ideas at his or her fingertips. Well, if this is what you think, are you in for a rude awakening, just as I was.

The first few weeks were a whirlwind of meetings, figuring out the number of students in each grade, generating and receiving numerous memos, reviewing dismissal and line-up strategies, planning fire drill routines, making bus schedules, making copies of performance standards for each grade, developing a code of behavior for students, arranging for picture day, distributing materials, giving out Metropolitan Transit Authority passes to the students who used the bus or subway, setting up—and in my case still teaching—math groups, distributing weekly report letters, setting up bulletin board schedules, and hand-delivering chancellor directives on merchandise requisitions to each teacher! As well, I had to count and distribute all of the math manuals and select a teacher to give out red ribbons against drug abuse.

And, in the midst of all this, I had to check each class to make sure that enough appropriately sized chairs were assigned to the respective classes! This basically summarizes my first few weeks as an acting AP. The work involved, as you can now imagine, was both daunting and exhausting.

In addition to the varied duties I was expected to carry out, there were the many interactions with the teachers and parents. When I had my own class it was easy to deal with the parents of my math lab students and also with the prep teachers whose classes came to my room. As AP, I had a far more difficult job. I had to deal with the teachers, paraprofessionals, lunchroom staff, custodial staff, and hundreds of parents in a professional and respectful manner. Because I had taught at P.S. 145 since 1965, I knew many of the parents as many had been to see me. The neighborhood was also a familiar place. I knew the local shopkeepers too. And that was a plus. Even though 105th Street and Amsterdam Avenue was one of the worst drug blocks in New York City at that time, believe it or not, I felt safe and welcome in the neighborhood.

It was my goal to be as visible as possible once I became AP. I was "all over the place," as one teacher said. I wanted the teachers and parents to know that I intended to make P.S. 145 a safe and productive learning environment. My principal and staff were very supportive. Their cooperation really helped me survive the year!

We developed a mission statement for our school. Our objectives were:

1. Each student will read twenty-five books or more. The younger students could have the books read to them.

2. Each reading will be followed by an activity.
3. We will focus on grammar and spelling, and obtain a schoolwide grammar guide to support language arts and enhance the writing process.
4. There will be bimonthly age-related writing projects, reports, narratives, poetry, etc.
5. We will improve math proficiency by using a variety of strategies.
   -Problem solving: Math Mindbenders with a new problem each week
   -Manipulatives
   -Workbooks
   -Math program, University of Chicago, TERC

In addition, we planned to develop:

1. A code of behavior for discipline
2. A weekly behavior report
3. Material to help students understand the curriculum for their grade
4. Handwriting books for all students
5. Schoolwide projects
6. A regular flow of positive feedback to students and teachers from me

Nonacademic Aspects of the AP Job

There are many things that they never taught us in college about teaching. The biggest surprise I encountered during this unbelievable journey as an acting AP was the unusual and varied nonacademic moments! In order to better convey my experience to the reader, let me share a portion of my daily journal.

September 16: -Called to Office because Sandy is crying—"It is too hot, Mrs. Storck."
September 17: -Parent came in to complain about a teacher hitting her son. Teacher claims a fly was on his head and she hit him to get it off! Teacher said she did not touch him. However, she removed his shirt because it was too hot!
September 18: -Note from teacher—Jerry needs an escort to Ms. X's room. He refused to go on by himself or with a partner.
September 21: -Sandy left the building with his mother. Mother refuses to let him have his class changed. Poor Sandy!
September 23: -Teacher wants Michelle or Simon out of her class!
   -A fifth grade teacher sent for me. Her girls are discussing who is a virgin.
   -Nail thrown at Donna by Larry.

September 24: -10:00AM Sheila left my room (third grade). Please go find her.

-11:00AM I had to go to the art class to watch a student.

-Mrs. B, the Principal, got a call from the Office of School Foods and Nutrition.—They were coming in 20 minutes and I had to meet them and then escort them to the lunchroom staff.

-12:30AM Brought Sheila back to her class. Fifth grade teacher called and said Wally was cursing in his class and he wanted me to come and get him.

September 28: -8:00AM Sunshine Committee meeting.

-Today Piano movers were coming. They will move piano from room 131 to the Auditorium. I have to check the top of the piano because it does not close properly.

-1:30-2:30 Discipline Assemblies. Discuss line up, lunchroom behavior and code of behavior.

-Kindergarten teachers upset about playground schedule and confused about rain or no rain policy. Canvassed kindergarten paraprofessionals for lunch duty—everything is okay—so cooperative.

-Cigarette and lighter left in 213. Inform Principal.

-1st grader Albert was under table and won't come out.

-Go outside at dismissal and show each class where they line up in the yard.

-Two teachers have verbal fight in the Office about career counseling.

-Teacher and parent have disagreement over dismissal routine.

-Albert and Fernando need therapy.

-Arnold bit a child in the leg.

-Carl swallowed a round gold thing.

October 2: -Complaint from social worker about the heat in School Based Support team's room. Spoke to custodial to fix it.

-Schedule change Garden Meeting—1:30.

-Fifth grade emergency problem. Ella can't read and cried about it. She feels no one loves her—poor self-esteem—teacher and I hug her and tell her she will get special help.

-Teacher needed a letter from her file for a tenure date.

-Diane threatened Jerry "I will cut your throat." Bring children to Principal.

-Accident report. Juan cut his head.

-Parents have a fight at 3:00 PM over a coat.

October 6: -Held breakfast for parents of fifth grade students. The topic of discussion was middle schools.

-Readers Digest called trying to push a gift program.

-Ray threw a book in his classroom because he got an N in line up.

-Jerome's mother came in to complain about his ripped jacket.

-Kindergarten child reportedly had an odor. Mother of the child came in to school and said her child smelled because of a ghost!

-Pouring rain at dismissal. Parents yelled at me about the rain. I replied that I am not God and a child then stated that I am only mortal.

October 8: -District called and wanted to make full classes in our school.

-Prepared pre-suspense letters for two students.

-I needed to be present at a Parents Association meeting.

-Father and mother of child are not together. Child wants his father to be part of his life but the father will not come in to see him.

-Child abuse case discovered. The school nurse will investigate.

-Note from kindergarten teacher to another teacher: "We have the wrong lunch form, do you have ours?" Can you help them find the correct form?

-Teacher giving math cluster was having a hard time about groups.

-Debra sleeps a lot, she has kidney problems. The medication is strong and she is only six-years old.

October 16: -Settled problem in a third grade class by changing seats of two arguing students

-Checked fifth grade bulletin board on limericks and found it was on farts.

-Fixed phone ringer in room 330.

-Called Atlantic Express Bus Company to get the pick up and drop off times for selected students.

-Teacher sent student to office because the student called the teacher stupid.

And, it was only October!

ELENA

Respect, Fairness, and Consistency

It starts on the first second of the first day when school begins in September. As the nervous five-year-olds tentatively step over the threshold into the classroom with their even more concerned parents behind them, the stage is set for the next ten months. A new village is created.

It took me a long time to understand that some kids come to school and really don't know about not yelling or hitting or poking or pestering or manners or mutual respect. And then, we want them to instantly, magically, know the rules. But, day by day, over and over again, they learn from an environment that provides consistency and constant reinforcement of the rules for our classroom village, for our classroom family, for our microcosm of social interaction.

They get to feel safe for six hours. They do not have to watch their backs. They will be protected and nurtured. It might not carry over into their non-school life every day, but a light will be ignited, for a new way to be, and maybe it will glimmer or sparkle or glow at unpredictable moments in their future.

Simple Rules

Respect, fairness, and consistency will be the simple yet complex rules for all, for the children, the parents, and the teacher. Yes, the teacher may not snack or chew gum or sip on coffee during the day if the kids can't.

No candy, no money, no home toys, especially little cars and Barbies. Before I realized the intoxicating effect of Barbie, kids would bring them to school and leave them in their book bags during the day. But it was like an underground unspoken communication; some of the girls would know it was *there*. They would fixate on getting to that special book bag during work centers, on the way to the bathroom, at lunchtime. Their focus was compromised for the whole day. It was like an addiction; Barbie was nearby. So, Barbie was banned from even entering. Other fad toys, also, had a draw over the years but none as strong as Barbie. Therefore, no home toys were permitted.

Our book bags, coats and hats, went right to the cubbies and stayed there until three o'clock. When we walked over the threshold into our classroom, everything belonged to our class family. It gave relief from territoriality. It gave a level playing field. It eliminates envy, fixating, hoarding. It promoted sharing and mutual caring for our family materials. It becomes a mindset for our village.

The Teaching Circle

The simple configuration of sitting in a circle on the rug is an ancient social tool, a circle of respect, a circle of fairness. There is no beginning or end, no front or back seat. We all have to look at one another. No playing around in the back because there is no back. We can watch each other sing and maybe some will learn the words from watching and listening to a child across the circle. We can watch and listen to each other talk and maybe a shy one will learn a new social cue.

We can hold hands with a neighbor. We can still see the teacher; she is in the circle too. We can see each other and notice the behaviors that are pleasant and kind and also the ones that are annoying and maybe learn not to copy them. The troublesome child also realizes that he or she is on display to all and sometimes might self-correct by watching appropriate behavior. The teaching circle is a very strong tool.

Partners of the Day: Eliminating the Cookie Factor

Kids in my kindergarten classes came in all different shapes, colors, and personalities. Some were always more charismatic than others. Some were cleaner. Some were funnier or happier or friendlier. But the bottom line always was that for six hours and twenty minutes we were a family, and it was my job to make sure it was a happy, safe, and respectful configuration. Not many adults would be able to survive six hours and twenty minutes in one kindergarten room with twenty-five other grown-ups, with one bathroom, perform appropriate if not challenging academic learning tasks, practice social skills, interact politely, share materials and space, and be able to maintain a happy, safe, and respectful environment until three o'clock came around. Yet, this is what we expect of twenty-five children every day. Many teachers get frustrated, angry, impatient, and even mean, when the kids cannot seem to get along by themselves without some guidance and without being taught some strategies of life.

Thus, the "partners of the day" concept was formed. Some kids only want to be around others who are like them. Some kids are equal opportunity classmates. Some are loners while some are magnets, some are gregarious, some shy or withdrawn. It was again my job to allow them all to experience one another in a nurturing and non authoritative way. A child cannot be made to be a new friend but a child can be encouraged to try something new.

So, in the safety, yet again, of the meeting circle, every morning we would perform the choosing of the partner of the day ritual. There was a pack of index cards with each child's name on a card. Every day, after the opening greeting songs, I would shuffle the cards and begin by holding up two cards for the class to observe and read. Those two children would stand up and walk to each other, look in each other's eyes, shake hands, and greet each other with the salutation, "We are partners today, let's not forget!" That's right, let's not forget because their teacher would most certainly forget all those partners (at the beginning of the year I would write them down). Kids have terrific memories and this was a helpful way to get involved in someone else's business.

Then we would proceed through the pack until each child had a partner. If, by attendance, there were an odd number of kids, the last three cards would be held up and those three would greet each other with "We are triplets today. Let's not forget."

The triplets would always be the caboose of our line when we were out and about in the school. By the second month of school, almost everyone had been each other's partner. No one ever fainted or died from having a partner that they did not really know or like. And on many, many occasions over the years, new friendships and bonds were formed, and those little five-year-olds were able to articulate that if they had not been partners of the day they would never have taken a chance on each other and they would have only stuck with their comfort zone friends.

Partners of the day seems like a simple procedure but it also had its academic component. It began simply with their names. Some came to kindergarten not being able to recognize their own names. So, in the beginning, I would read out the names. In this manner, those that could not read their names were not embarrassed and also the others began to build the sight vocabulary of their classmates' names. They began to put faces to the names. This was helped by the name tags that the kids wore for the first week of school. Children have a better facility at remembering names than their aging teachers do.

Slowly, the calling of the names stopped and the cards were just held up and the kids had to be attentive to reading their own names. The rule of the ritual was that you could not call anyone else's name out or poke your neighbor into attentiveness. Sometimes, it really was quite funny as we sat in the circle for what seemed an endless time waiting for the appropriate child to pop up. It was all done in good humor.

The kids had to pop up with enthusiasm, not roll slowly up or crawl to each other. The concept was to be a joyful start of the day with an energetic beat.

So, partners of the day was a great organizational tool for walking to and from lunch, out to the play yard, to the school library, computer lab, and auditorium. It took away the territoriality and obsessions of having only one best friend. It leveled the playing field and was safe and inclusive. No one was ever left out. There was no negotiation, the line just formed.

As the year progressed, the first name cards were replaced with last names, initials, phone numbers, addresses, favorite dinosaurs, favorite foods, etc. The group reading vocabulary was ever expanding.

A second pack of name cards was used for the sign-in chart everyday. As the children arrived, they moved their own cards from out to in. This was an easy sorting tool for attendance and, again, an interactive, easy, and no offensive way for the five-year-olds to mind each other's business. As the partner of the day cards changed to last names, etc., the sign-in cards also changed. They were bombarded with active vocabulary.

Partners of the day was accompanied by "Kid of the Day."

On a permanent chart near the front of the room, was a list of all the kids' names (in the beginning, it was first names, then became last names, etc.). It was an alphabetical list. Later in the year, they realized what alphabetical was without even being told. So, instead of having kid of the month or week or year—yikes!—every twenty-five days (of course, depending on the number of kids in the class) a kid would have a chance to be Kid of the Day.

The Kid of the Day was the line leader, took important papers to the office, held the doors, helped with special tasks, counted the kids at circle time, presented the opening report about the calendar, weather, and the number line of how many days we had been in school. They had to remember their responsibilities. It was a big job. They loved it. They would negotiate ways of how to not miss their turn if they had to be absent for a doctor's appointment. It was also an attendance tool. Many times, parents would report that their child had to come to school because it was their turn to be Kid of the Day. But, alas, if you were absent on your day, it went to the next kid. That was always fun to figure out, especially on snow days. It was a lucky kid who got his or her turn much earlier than expected because of the weather. Over the years, Kid of the Day began to take on a life of its own. Kids talked about probability and speculated on what day their next turn would be. They became masters of the calendar. Lots of higher level thinking came out of this simple classroom tool.

But the best link between partner of the day and Kid of the Day was that if you were the partner of the Kid of the Day you got to be the line leader too!

Appropriate and Acceptable

It is important to establish a class language with a working vocabulary that is understood by all. By highlighting an expectation of excellence rather than harping on negative behavior, using the words "appropriate" and "acceptable" evolved into a great kindergarten management tool. Instead of thousands of no no no's all day long, I would comment on a job well done, kind words, thoughtful gestures, etc. It became a deductive sort of reasoning. When someone grabbed a toy or yelled at a classmate, for instance, I would say, sometimes strongly or sometimes softly, "That's not acceptable," or "That was not appropriate." And, believe it or not, by October, the kids were saying it to each other in appropriate ways. The offending kids did not like to hear it and mostly would self-correct, and the offended kids would feel the power of a few well-placed words. This, of course, spilled over into the homes and many a parent came to me over the years to tell me that they had been scolded for behavior that was deemed not acceptable by their five-year-olds. And, they would usually admit, it indeed was true.

No emotional, physical, or verbal violence in the classroom or school ever ever ever!

(See above about acceptable). One year during our extensive examination of the great work of Dr. Martin Luther King, Jr., we came up with a synopsis of the importance of his great work—namely, Dr. King worked nonviolently to change the bad rules. One kid who had a contentious relationship with her mother about drinking her milk at dinnertime announced, with the full bravado of an empowered five-year-old, that she was not going to drink her milk *because* Dr. King fought to change the bad rules. She had taken our discussions seriously. It was not until the next morning that the argument was settled. Her exasperated mother asked me to set it straight so I very seriously announced that Dr. King thought it was a good rule for kids to drink their milk. I hope he did but then there is the issue of lactose intolerance!

Good-bye Song

We opened each day with a meeting circle with the same songs of greeting. Some songs were added or removed as the seasons changed. And, likewise, we closed each day with songs of farewell. The kids would gather their stuff from the cubbies and put on their coats or sweaters and sit in the circle, and right before the parents appeared at the door for pick up, we would sing our songs of hope and farewell until the next morning. We alternated through a collection of about ten songs; they would know which one by the introductions played on the piano. Some were traditional children's songs, some from rock and roll, some funny or heartfelt. As the parents appeared, each kid in turn would change their name card to the "out" side and the day would end until we would be together tomorrow again.

Keeping the Door Open

Teaching is a juggling act; that is for sure. Negotiating parents, administrators, colleagues and students is not for the weak at heart. They never told (not to mention counseled) us in our methods courses in college or at staff development about the logistics or politics of running a successful classroom environment. And on top of this task we also had to be nurturing educators. Keeping one's classroom door open is sometimes a magic trick and a sleight of hand. It is an invitation to visit but it is also an advertisement to overzealous administrators and coaches that there is nothing in this room to worry about because why would the door be open if there was something to hide. So, if you are doing an excellent job with your students according to your own standards, even though it might not be what the administrators want, keep your door open and they will mostly leave you alone. They will go skulking around the doors that are closed because if the door is closed they can peek through that small door window unannounced, and perhaps find some violations of the bureaucratic rules.

But if you are following your own heart and doing great work in a nurturing and interesting way, and your door is open, they cannot skulk at the little window. You will see them at the corner of the door with their clipboards and pens and then you will promptly and enthusiastically announce to your children, "Hey kids, look, Principal Madam is here to visit us (of course, not spy on us). Isn't that great? Come on in, Principal Madam, come and join a group or come sing a song with us or get your hands wet at water experimentation or help that group clean out the hamster's cage or come and read us a story (you used to be great at that, maybe) or it would be great if you could take a group to the bathroom or clean up where this little one just threw up." The invitations to participate could be endless. And, guess what, *they never accept*, unless they are authentic educators as well, in which case there probably is peace in the school anyway. They will smile and make their exit as quickly as possible.

Keeping the door open is also a useful tool with the parents. Parents usually feel that their children are being well taught and well cared for if the door is open. Parents want to be welcomed and want to be a part of their children's education. Work and other life issues, unfortunately, are a barrier to involvement. You want the parents to be your allies and supporters. Unlike the backwards psychology of administrators, you don't want parents to be uninvolved, so the wider open the door and the invitation, the better the communication. Some parents come with great gifts of organization or nurturing or cooking or other helpful talents.

Unfortunately and realistically, there are parents whom you wish would go away. In that case, see above, the tactic used with the annoying administrator will work. Give them a job, a group, a responsibility, and they usually discover other pressing things to do during the day. All parents want the best for their kids; some just need extra handling. You will find that if the parents are assured that things are safe and sound, they will eventually trust you enough to leave you alone. It takes longer with some.

Spreading the word is also helped by leaving the door open. New teachers, and sometimes old teachers, hear or see through that open door that interesting things are happening inside. They hear the music, the singing. They might smell the enticing aromas of the cooking project or spot those colorful candied gingerbread houses on the front table—a deliberate display. Sometimes, the curious will come in and ask what's going on and join right in. Sometimes, the shy will linger at the door, not wanting to be a bother or interfere. Spread the word; a teachable moment for your colleagues is at hand.

There used to be two new teachers who were friends who would wander into my room when they had a common prep together. They would never come alone. At first, they would just linger in the doorway. Little by little, just like kids, they would come in a little more and stand in the corner by the door and watch whatever was going on, circle time, singing, a writing workshop, work centers. They would just watch quietly.

Then, they progressed towards coming in and sitting down and watching. They might stay for a few minutes or ten or twenty minutes. They would never interrupt me or chat. Finally, after months of doing this, they finally told me that they liked coming in to just soak up the aura and essence of my room and the kids. They felt it gave them a lift for the rest of the day; the strength to go on and do their own good work. Over the years, I had many types of visiting colleagues. Some would just walk in look around and walk out. Some (including one beloved principal) would sit in the comfy chair as an escape from the rest of their day for a while. Some were curious about my different technique. Some went on to become my dearest friends. All of this from taking a peek in an open door.

JACKQUELYNN

I entered teaching late in my work career. It began when I finally received my BA in international studies. Finding the job market sparse and because of my lack of a second language, I was eager to leave the foundation where I had been working for sixteen years. There is a part of me that believes in fate. I had briefly gone back into the foundation field and realized I was making no change. One Sunday, I happened to be browsing the *New York Times*, and saw that Fordham University was advertising a unique Fellowship Master's Mentoring Program in education. Everything seemed to fall into place like the missing pieces of a puzzle. I won the Fellowship and was immediately placed into a parochial third-grade classroom.

I am sure I made a lot of mistakes in that first year. But I seemed to remember what good teaching was, through memories of a wonderful teacher I had in elementary school. I was fortunate to have her in fourth and sixth grades. I believe she greatly influenced me, particularly in her style of teaching. What I remembered of her class was that she made it interesting, challenging, and fun. I never remembered being sad or bored in her class. She seemed to open the doors to a world of history, geography. She inspired a love of reading in me.

Once in the education field, I found I had a thirst that could not be quenched. I attended workshops after school, on Saturdays, and during the summers. I tried to bring workable examples back into my classroom. In my later teaching years, the Internet became a vital tool in planning my lessons and curricula. As I reread this during our editing stage, I realized what worked for me was having a wonderful role model and the constant honing of my craft. I tried to seek out the teachers that were innovative and sharing. I also realized I sacrificed a lot of personal and private time.

My room was a reflection of children's learning, i.e., inquiry-based, thematic units. I developed the routine of welcoming parents into the classroom. I found out early on that parents welcomed invitation so that they could observe their child in a positive environment. I also realized that, in that positive light, children were at their best and eager to impart their knowledge. So often, the only contact outside of parent/teacher conferences was negative contact. Parents observed their young authors and publishers, toured class museums, attended plays, puppet shows, and poetry readings. What worked for me was encouraging parent involvement and continuous open dialogue about our classroom. It takes a village to raise a child. Parents and teachers are an essential part of the village. What also worked for me was maintaining a professional but welcoming attitude towards the administration. The administration and their visitors were always welcomed in my classroom. However, it seemed that the more you welcomed them the less frequently they involved themselves.

What worked for me was having my students make connections in the world outside of the classroom, through field trips and school wide cultural activities. What worked well for me was being a team player, participating in professional and curriculum development, being a grade leader and a school-based committee participant, and offering constructive ideas and criticism, developing a bookroom for guided reading materials for grades K through five, organizing early childhood competitive games, and researching scholarships for private school candidates, to name a few.

I believe a teacher's personality is reflected in the classroom. What may work for one teacher may or may not work for another. What might work for one child might not work for the next. Therefore, the new policy of everyone on the same page at the same time is doomed to fail. Teaching is an evolving process.

Reading in My Classroom

As each year began, my excitement grew at the prospect of sharing, exploring, and opening the world of reading to my students. My career in the elementary school focused on grades one to three. First graders coming from kindergarten came with some knowledge of the alphabet and the connecting sounds. Generally, they knew the days of the week, months in a year, names of colors, counting of numbers, and directional words. They had a sense of story and had been exposed to formal literacy. Occasionally, you received a child that had not been to day care or kindergarten. They sat, somewhat attentively, as you began the process of teaching them to read. They were as eager as you to begin the adventure.

Each year, I prepared the room with each child's name on a card placed on his or her desk. The names were also placed underneath the room alphabet beginning with the first letter of their name, for example, A's = Alex, Alison, Alfred, etc. Although there was a proliferation of materials on the market, I learned that some things were better than others and so many things could be teacher-made.

During the first weeks of school, I concentrated on the alphabet and its sounds, as a review, and to teach students who had not been exposed. Later on, students made individual ones. Each morning, as students settled, we began "Today's News" during Circle Time. This consisted of using simple sentences to talk about the day, the weather. Each day, a child would contribute a personal sentence to our news. The news helped reinforce the alphabet, since we would circle or underline the letters or word that was our focus for the day or week. We read our news as a group and then individually. This news was eventually copied in their notebooks as an exercise in forming letters, and writing and reading sentences. I encouraged them to write individual sentences. Later, the children would share their work. This small and consistent routine also included using the basic sight words. It was their start on the road to reading. Picture-word cards, lots of poetry, songs, illustration of stories, and the labeling of everyday objects resulted in a room rich in print. Early in the term, we included the print that children saw in their everyday environment—tops of cereal boxes, food containers, advertisements of fast food stores, beverages, etc. We made lists, all kinds of lists of names, food, places, and things. I began putting these lists in alphabetical order on the closet bulletin boards. These later became known as "Word Walls."

Reading came quickly to some, slower to others. As the term progressed, I introduced appropriate reading material. Usually, I used small eight-page readers with simple words. I found time to systematically sit with students to listen as they struggled to "break the code."

I drew heavily on the classic fairy tales that students could retell and illustrate. Often, we retold the story and worked together in groups, illustrating it on chart paper. Then, a sentence would be pasted underneath the picture.

Once displayed along the walls, students used attractive "pointers" to "read the room."

The room was essentially a hands-on environment, bustling with meaningful activities. I seized every opportunity to create a teachable moment.

As I moved into the second- and third-grade Gifted and Talented Class, the activities became more sophisticated. Each week we read a third-grade version of *Times Magazine*, a children's periodical, *Storyworks*, a daily newspaper, and a variety of genres from our class library. At the beginning of the year, this reading material was a challenge. However, by the end, students were able to read at length individually, in pairs, in groups.

Each year our school celebrated Poetry Month. Throughout the year, students worked on haiku, limericks, acrostic poems, and rhyme. Word puzzles, spelling games, and vocabulary building served as reinforcement to strengthen reading skills. Students created their own individual newspapers and wrote book reports that reflected their independent reading. We were fortunate to have a great anthology provided by the school.

We took class trips to museums, theatres, and restoration projects. The students reflected on these trips in writing and gave oral reports. They built museums and made reproductions of artifacts of Egypt and China. As authors, they wrote stories, made books, and published them in handmade books they shared during publishing parties.

Teaching reading to new readers has been an unexplainable joy. I remember in my early years of teaching sitting with little Samantha. She struggled and struggled. One day in early May, as we sat together, she slowly began to read . . . sentence after sentence. I stopped at the end and asked, "Samantha, when did you learn to read?" Her reply was simply the widest smile of joy I had ever seen. It is a memory I hold on to.

The Literacy Lab

As an outgrowth of my classroom activities, my principal asked if I would be willing to institute a Literacy Lab. This lab would take the same activities from my classroom used to enhance and enrich the encouragement of reading, and make them available to a larger population. The lab also served as a push in model with the English as Second Language (ESL) teacher, Samantha Jory.

First and second grades were the primary targets. They came twice a week. Several third-grade classes were also chosen. When I look back at photos of the two years in the lab, I remember that the room was flooded with reading activities, samples of work and excitement. Ideally, teachers and paraprofessionals accompanied the classes. The lab was a rich environment with three or four adults assisting children who were able to receive more 1:1 attention than they did ordinarily. It was wonderful having the extra hands. Unfortunately, some teachers or paraprofessionals saw it as a prep period and would disappear until the end of the period. I guess one can never achieve 100 percent cooperation.

Activities and practice modeled and demonstrated in the lab were designed to be carried over and implemented in the classrooms. This meant poetry, matching words to pictures, retelling of stories, making books about these same stories, patterning, working in themes, and much more. The ESL teacher was extremely innovative in helping to plan activities beneficial to second language students. As a team we worked with teachers to coordinate with planning in their classrooms.

Working with lots of nursery rhymes, and classic fairy tales and stories, we often combined art in the activities. A follow-up to "The Gingerbread Man" included making gingerbread houses. My advice to readers, however, is to first really think through such activities. I calculated that we made almost 400 gingerbread houses in one week.

The second year of the lab yielded very different results. They moved the lab from the first and second grades to the third and fourth grades. The lab coordinated activities to match the social studies and science themes in the classroom. There was a focus on writing skills, as well as reading. The ESL teacher was asked to split her time with individual students and the lab. In general, what worked well in the lower grades did not necessarily translate likewise to the upper grades. There just did not seem to be the same enthusiasm from students at this age.

So I requested a return to the classroom and began teaching second- and third-grade Gifted and Talented classes.

On reflection, I took great pride in the Literacy Lab model I created for the first and second grades. I believe it was also a concrete model for the ESL students who were able to participate in the class without being pulled out. Samantha and I later demonstrated the model at a Teacher's College TESOL conference.

Self-Reflection

As a new, enthusiastic teacher I wanted to be the very best at this new career I had chosen. I meticulously prepared lesson plans, bought all kinds of materials for my classroom, practically lived in Barnes & Noble, Bank Street Bookstore, and Strand Book Store. The first year as a teacher, I calculated the money spent and it totaled over $2,700. After that, I stopped calculating! I certainly, over the years, became the butt of jokes if someone needed materials— "Ask Jackie!"

I scoured through catalogs, and later, when I acquired Internet access, spent hours late into the early morning, looking at other schools, lesson plans, theories, examples of activities. I did so to keep my students motivated and enthusiastic. But, most importantly, I did so to quench my thirst of knowledge.

When I entered P.S. 145, our school district offered a multitude of free after-school workshops. Some were required, most were not. Frequently, these workshops gave new materials and samples of literature, science kits, or math manipulatives. Good workshops were those offering hands-on activities, and samples of student work. I remember trekking out to Long Island one Saturday to a Wright Group seminar.

I continued doing this for about two or three years. It was good for networking with other teachers. But I did notice that there was never anyone from my school or district attending. Often I asked colleagues to join, but people do not often want to give up their personal time. I do acknowledge that many had families, but I met so many other teachers at these workshops who had families too. On the other hand, many teachers had students come to their homes for group activities they could not have accomplished in the classroom.

At Fordham University, I was once told that as a teacher you were like the clown at the circus. A beginning clown has a small bag of tricks. However, each year the bag gets larger and larger. So, in essence, those early years of my teaching career were spent filling my own bag.

Slowly, I began to see what was working and what was not. I realized my own personal working style demanded order in the classroom. I developed a routine for entering the room and settling down in the classroom and for completing the many mandated administrative tasks. I found that having my students start with an activity that required writing (journaling, poetry, daily news, etc.) calmed them as they transitioned from schoolyard to classroom. It gave me time to clear my head, assess the mood of the students, and deal with parental and medical emergencies. I found that, despite all the suggested class procedures, this worked best for me.

As a teacher, I always kept an open door policy regarding parents. They were invited to visit and were welcomed. Many teachers have closed door policies because they feel parents will interfere. I have often found if parents became too much of a nuisance, assigning them a classroom job usually led to infrequent visits. Generally, parents who want to be involved are committed.

What worked for me was an enthusiastic, busy, and bustling classroom. Students were always involved, as they should be, in the learning process. I too was often the student. I do not think one can be an effective teacher without becoming the student. Questioning, seeking, learning, and participating give one an insight into teaching that cannot be obtained through books.

I remember ordering a butterfly kit. I set it up and each day rushed in to see the new emerging life. When they embarked from their cocoons, I was probably more excited than the students. As a teacher, I think, I did so much learning. That constant self-learning was what worked for me.

School Spirit, School Participation

A sense of community exists in every school. It begins in the classroom and should filter throughout the school. Teachers often complain that students are not motivated. Motivation can often take place in the classroom, as well as in auxiliary classrooms: art, library, science, computer, and gym.

Students are often at their best when they are working towards a goal. I found in my own classroom, particularly, when working on thematic units, that culminating activities, shared with fellow grades and the school, assured a measure of success. These culminating activities also allowed me to assess what the students had actually learned.

Our classroom participated in developing model museums, with students serving as docents. Students worked on model irrigation systems, historic tombs, water clocks, and map making intended for Egypt. We studied and exhibited multicultural bookmaking, and built model rooms and city blocks, created monster masks, wrote creative endings for fairy tales, and challenged writers to have characters of two different stories meet each other. In the early fall, we began plant study by sprouting beans, planting them, transferring them into the school garden, and later harvesting beans. One year, we built terrariums from soda bottles. Most of this work was shared with other classes.

My class participated in school contests, especially ones conducted by the librarian. The weekly meeting in the library fostered the growth of library and research skills. It also added critical thinking to the read-aloud in the library. The librarian also conducted poetry and storytelling contests that were not only school wide but regional as well.

One year, after watching the upper classes participate in mock Olympics in the schoolyard and trying to figure out why the lower grades had nothing comparable, I began researching other kinds of school Olympics and we instituted The Mother Goose Games. Teachers dressed as favorite Mother Goose characters, and age-appropriate competitive activities took place in the school yard: carrying plastic eggs on spoons, Simple Simon balance the pie plate, etc. All participants received certificates. This activity brought out parents to cheer for students.

Of course, there are many teachers who will not participate. This causes friction and derision among both the students and staff as well. It is hard for them to see their peers apparently having fun while they are not. It goes back acknowledging, "It's about the children."

I looked forward to the auditorium presentations from other classes. One year, my class adapted *Mufaro's Beautiful Daughters.* Students learned dialogue, songs, dances, and crafted stage sets and artwork. This is an area where listening skills, following directions, and social skills are developed. It is hard, but rewarding work.

I encouraged my students to join the school chorale group. It was perhaps inconvenient for me when they needed to leave class for rehearsals. However, there was the thoughtfulness of the director, who arranged her rehearsals during the last period of the school day. This time proved valuable to the remaining students, who were able to complete projects or small-group work during that period.

School, ultimately, is for the students. Without them, we would not be there.

URSULA

Multiage Classroom

There almost always were children in our school who did not quite fit in with their classmates. Some were so quiet, they were hardly noticed. Others spent an amazing amount of time avoiding being in class, frequenting bathrooms and hallways. Some children caused regular disturbances in their classroom.

One of the latter, a fifth grader, spent many days in my kindergarten classroom as a visitor and "helper" in the weeks before his graduation from elementary school. Any more suspensions on his record would have automatically made him a holdover.

I was surprised how well Timmy fit into our kindergarten class. He loved our snacks, loved our mini naps. He enjoyed playing with the five- and six-year-olds. He was very nice to them. The nurturing, nonthreatening, low-stress environment in my kindergarten classroom seemed to suit him well. Timmy's home life was quite stressful. He lived with his elderly father, who was rather ill, in a homeless shelter. The father depended on Timmy almost as much as Timmy depended on him.

To keep Timmy busy and maintain the pretense of academic work for him, I asked him to make an alphabet book for the children, including illustrations, definitions, and descriptions of the objects he chose for each letter. Every day,

Timmy worked on the alphabet book, and every day during our class meeting he gave us an update on his progress. When his book was finally finished, his biggest wish was to show it to the principal. He was so proud of himself. He had done a fine job. He received many compliments on it and I arranged for him to read it to other kindergarten and first-grade classes.

Somehow, within the structure of our kindergarten environment, we met Timmy's needs. We fed him when he was hungry, let him sleep when he needed to, and accepted him without making fun of his chubbiness or his odd clothing. He happily abided by our class rules: be kind to each other, clean up after yourself, and keep your noise at a level where you don't disturb others. We also gave him the opportunity to contribute to our classroom community, and we acknowledged his contribution on a regular basis. At the end of the school year, Timmy graduated. On his graduation day, he came running to our classroom, shirttails flying, and necktie in hand. He wanted me to tie it for him and make sure that he looked all right. The kindergartners gathered around us, witnessing this important moment in Timmy's life. "Don't worry kids, I'll be back in the afternoon" were his words as he went off to his graduation.

After my experience with Timmy, I proposed to the administration to set up a multiage classroom for children like Timmy. It would be for children who had difficulties functioning in their regular classroom but who should not be in a special education class either. I had always wanted to teach in an old-fashioned "little red schoolhouse" and now saw an opportunity to create one within our school. The administration presented the idea to the teaching staff who were quite enthusiastic. Before long, the class roster for the proposed first- through third-grade was completed. It was, however, not so easy to convince some of the parents of the children assigned to my nongraded class. "She is a good teacher, this will be beneficial for your child, she will have an assistant and it will be a small class," were some of the arguments the principal made to reluctant parents. She also guaranteed the parents the option to have their child removed if they did not like the class. And, so, I had my little red schoolhouse within our school.

During my summer vacation, I looked for professional literature on multiage classrooms but found very little. The state of Kentucky, at one time, wanted to implement multiage classrooms in all of its schools but met with resistance from its teachers' union and had to give up the idea. "Too much work" had been the argument against it. They had planned on combining just two grades. We already had this at our school and it was called a "bridge class." It usually occurred for organizational reasons and was a way for the administration to come up with the right number of students per class. At one time, the G&T (Gifted and Talented) program at our school was set up that way, with three classes for six grade levels. From the point of a parent, whose child had participated in the program, it had worked very well. When the number of G&T students at the school increased, the bridge classes disappeared without any pedagogical discourse about their advantage for students.

I traveled to Wisconsin and South Dakota that summer of 1997 and during my travels I looked for one room schoolhouses. There was still one in operation on one of the Apostle Islands in Lake Superior. The school was looking for a new teacher and from what I heard quite a few teachers had applied. But most of the little schoolhouses, if they were still around, had been turned into museums. I visited a few of them. In the old days of the one-room schoolhouse, students desks were almost always attached to the floor, arranged in rows with the smallest children seated in front of the classroom and the larger, older students in the back. In one, I saw the students' desks arranged around the perimeter of the room, facing toward the walls and windows, but that was the exception. In any case, the seating arrangements did not indicate that students of different grades worked together; rather that they had been separated into grade levels within the school.

In South Dakota, I had the opportunity to talk to a former student of a one-room schoolhouse. He thought that he had received a good education. He based his opinion on how well his education had prepared him for his life. He was a successful rancher raising hundreds of beef cattle. He commented that he had learned to work independently. A teacher who had taught in a one-room schoolhouse said that her students, "while listening to the lessons taught to the other grades, got either a review of what they had already learned or a taste of what came next." These days we call this spiraling and peripheral learning. Most math programs incorporate it in their curriculum.

Invigorated by my summer's research, I came back to school a few days early to set up my classroom. I needed a variety of furniture to accommodate different-sized children. I set up three large tables, one for each grade, a kitchen area with a small fridge, hot plate, and waffle iron, and a comfortable library and reading area with books appropriate for all three grade levels. Later, the kitchen and library areas were frequently reorganized by the students. They liked to make them look nice or, as one of the students put it, "We have to have style!" I set up computer stations along the wall in the back of the room and designated a large carpeted area for our class meetings and for block building. Since the students were encouraged to work on their block building continuously during the week, by Tuesday we usually had to move our meeting to another part of the room. We had a class set of clipboards we called our "lap desks." On the clipboards, the children could do their work anywhere, even in the park. Besides the blackboard, I used large chart paper for many of my lessons. Clipboards, chart stands, and children well trained to move their chairs made for a very fluid use of our classroom space, and made it easy for me to arrange my students into various learning groups.

Implementing a Multiage Classroom

At the beginning of the school year we learned about the history of the one-room schoolhouse. I found a lovely children's book for us in the series "Historic Communities," with the title *A One Room School* by Bobbie Kalman. We also explored references to one-room schoolhouses in children's literature, for example in the *Little House on the Prairie* series by Laura Ingalls Wilder. I wanted to make sure that the children felt comfortable with their multiage classroom by providing examples of similar school situations. I also wanted them to understand and be able to explain how it worked, and its benefits to their friends and families. I should not have worried. My students almost immediately felt happy in their new classroom. Here is an entry from one of their journals. "Today I helped Jessie with her writing. She reminds me of my little sister. I liked helping her. Helping her made me feel happy." Instead of competing with each other, the children appreciated their abilities and the help they could provide for each other. Our classroom was about learning, not about who finished first or who was the smartest. Accordingly, there was less stress, less posturing, and less acting out in the classroom. None of the parents asked to have their child transferred out of the class.

There were surprisingly many learning activities that all three grades could do together, like journal writing, quiet reading, or computation practice. For computation practice, I usually put three columns on the board, one for each grade. The third graders had to do all three, the second graders two, and the first graders one. This was a very popular activity, especially for the older kids. Starting out with easy computation problems somehow made the hard ones at the end easier. Some first- and second-graders liked to do the problems above their grade level.

Art, music, and social studies also were whole-group activities. Specific reading and math instructions were done in small groups, reading practice often was done in pairs. Trips were so much easier and a lot more fun with this multiage group. We were like a big family, the older children holding the hands of the smaller ones and helping them along.

We had a piano in our classroom—what a treasure! It became a very important part of our little school community. A former teacher and pianist volunteered her time to give the students piano lessons. Once a week, she met with a small group during their lunch hour. Those students then became the teachers for the other students. During any given school day, there was almost always somebody practicing at the piano. During our daily morning circle, one of the students accompanied us on the piano. At the end of the school year, we gave a recital. It was a wonderful experience. Some of the parents had never heard their children play and were surprised and moved by their child's performance.

During our class meetings, the children learned to identify their own and each other's strength with games like "name three good things about the child who is sitting next to you." Our vocabulary for positive descriptive words increased as we became more and more adept in describing each other's talents and qualities.

As I got to know my students better, I made some interesting observations about the children who had been recommended for my class. About one-third of the children were in foster care. An unusually high number of the children in the class were left-handed. Many of the children needed glasses or had other vision problems. I'll always be thankful to the Children's Aid Society for generously providing free vision screening and glasses for our children and for not having the same rules as Medicare, one pair of glasses per child per year. Children lose and break their glasses frequently. They and their teachers should not be punished for it by having to do without.

I also observed that with less stress in their lives the students' learning was explosive. Children are amazing. Often, they find their own way through the labyrinth of their learning difficulties if given the time, food, and rest they need to function. Of course, in addition, some children require and *deserve* help with specific learning disabilities.

We continued with the program for three years, until I left for my Peace Corps tour in Uganda. I consider those three years among my happiest as a teacher. Most of the parents were pleased with the progress of their children. They also appreciated that their children were happy to go to school each day. Ms. Budd, our principal, complimented me at the end of the school year. "Ursula," she said, "you gave the children back their childhood."

Our Classroom Community

At the beginning of each school year, I made a conscious effort to create a sense of community within my classroom. We started by getting to know and accept each other. With songs and games, we learned each other's names, and introduced ourselves to the group.

In our classroom community, everybody had equal rights and equal responsibilities. It is not unusual to hear a teacher say, "If only so-and-so wasn't in my class." Imagine being that child! Imagine being that child's classmate! The constant fear of rejection, the worry of defying the teacher when interacting kindly with this child! I used to say to myself that whoever walks through my classroom door, on that first day of school, is my very special student. With the snotty nose, pants too long, shoelaces untied, unsharpened pencil, mother not too keen on me being her child's teacher, they would still be mine to love and to teach. Some teachers say "you can't love them all." But love is not a feeling, love is a recipe for thinking and acting, its opposite is rejection.

There are many ways to assure that all students have opportunities to contribute to their classroom community. Here are some I used in my classroom: Kid of the Day, as described by Elena, the old fashioned Show and Tell, as well as classroom jobs. Some of the jobs in my classroom were cleaning out our pet rabbit's cage, accompanying the class on the piano during morning circle, practicing reading with another classmate, checking math computation for each other, or preparing our waffles on Friday mornings. Preparing and sharing food is probably the oldest and most essential way to foster and celebrate community spirit.

The children always liked to have jobs. Some jobs, of course, were more popular than others. That's why we rotated them. We also, as a community, gave the students feedback on their job performances and, if necessary, made suggestions for improvement.

Setting Goals

At the beginning of the school year, I often asked my students: "What do you think you will learn this year?" I was always amazed at their answers. Children often have a good sense of "what's next." They also are aware that there is a learning agenda for them. In order for the children to set and meet goals for themselves, they have to know exactly what is expected of them.

During the school year we regularly reviewed our goals and took stock of our accomplishments. In order for the students to succeed, we have to let them take ownership of their learning. This is impossible under the new rule that everyone be on the same page at the same time. A good classroom community helps students to identify and celebrate their progress. And yes, "all students can and do learn," to quote Myra Langford, a former teacher and assistant principal at P.S. 145. "It's just a matter of proper acknowledgement."

Class Rules

On the first day of school, I would introduce our class rules. They were very simple and yet surprisingly comprehensive. These were our rules: You have to be kind. You must clean up after yourselves. And your noise level must not disturb others.

It was easy for the children to remember and to agree to these three, simple rules. Some teachers develop class rules with their students as part of the community building process. I do not recommend it. It is a bit like opening Pandora's Box. One easily ends up with a long list of don'ts, with a strong focus on negative behavior. Imagine walking into a classroom and seeing a large poster, "Our Class Rules." And yes, I have seen them, starting and ending with don'ts. Don't hit each other, don't push each other down, don't be late for school, don't disrespect each other's property, don't curse or use the "f" word, etc., etc. With such a list of negative behavior prominently displayed in the classroom, the teacher inadvertently advertises such behavior.

Children want to know what happens should they break the rules. We mainly just talked about it. Not "Why did you do this?" but instead, "Was this a kind thing to do?" "Why not?" "What do you need to do next?" "How can you fix your mistake?" We focused on a positive solution.

Community Rituals

Daily rituals are very important in community building. They keep the community on track, set sign posts, and create a common community language. Rituals are a response to the needs of a particular community.

Each morning, we started our day by gathering in a circle. We greeted each other and shared important news, about a new baby at home, perhaps, or a visiting grandparent. We passed out bread, carefully cut into equal pieces by one of the students and served in a special little basket. This sharing of bread had started accidentally but soon became something of a class trademark.

I was running late one morning. While guiding the students into the classroom, I hurriedly tried to eat a breakfast roll. The students looked both surprised and amused to see their teacher finishing breakfast after the bell, until one of them asked, "Teacher, can I have some bread too?" How could I say no to a child asking for bread? Soon, more little hands reached out and there went my breakfast. The next day, I bought two rolls to school for the children. The children were actually a little hungry. Not all of them had eaten breakfast even though the school had a free breakfast program. I bought a bread basket for the classroom and added the job of preparing the bread each morning to our job chart. I also discovered a bakery in the neighborhood where I could get two loaves of bread for the price of one after 8:00 p.m. That helped with the expense. We already knew a song that perfectly suited the occasion, "Peace is the bread we break," from the *Children's Songs for a Friendly Planet* songbook. That made our sharing ceremony complete. On

Fridays, for a special treat, we served our renowned waffles. Often, we shared them with other people in the school. This gave the students the opportunity to contribute to the larger school community.

Participating in and experiencing a positive classroom community is crucial for the students' academic success. It also teaches each child how to be a mensch, or a good person.

Parents' Club

It was the first day of school and one of those beautiful, bright, early autumn days in New York City. All the teachers were out in the yard, gathering their students for their new classes. I was at my assigned spot in the yard, class sign and class list in hand, and meeting my new students and their parents. I was teaching first grade.

The first day of first grade is such a very special day. To the brand new first grader, it seems that he or she has been waiting for this very moment all of their life. For the parents too, this is a big event, a big step for their child, and one that will affect the entire family.

Memories of my own first day of school came back to me. My father, who had taken off a few hours from work, my mother, my grandparents, and my godmother all accompanied me. I was given a huge, cone-shaped paper bag, beautifully decorated and almost as tall as I was. It was called a *schultuete* and was packed with goodies and school supplies. I barely could carry it; it was so big. I proudly carried my new schoolbag, in it a yet unscratched, smooth, dark black slate and a hand-crocheted eraser, made by my mother, with a long string attached. That string was there, so that it could be hung out of the schoolbag and air-dried on my way home. Clutching my *schultuete*, and encircled by my family, I bravely entered the big school.

Now here I was gathering my new first graders, with the smell of their morning scrubs still on their faces, and their brand new, still stiff school clothes. They proudly carried their brand new book bags that contained an assortment of school supplies. Later, we would sort through them, admire them, and decide which ones to keep at school or at home. Some of their pants and sweaters were rolled up at the cuffs or sleeves, definitely bought for growing into during the year. Children at that age grow so very fast.

The children were busy, shuffling around in their new shoes, often careful not to get them dirty. Smiling at each other, they recognized a face here or there from kindergarten or nursery school. Some were more shy, still clinging to their parents. Yet others were already asking the teacher their first question, a typical one being "Are we going to have homework?" For at that point in their lives, "having homework" was symbolic for belonging to the big world.

As a teacher and parent, I have very mixed feelings about homework, and as a child I often said, "I would love school if it were not for the homework." But on this lovely morning, I smiled at the eager six-year-old and assured him, "Yes, indeed, you will have homework, because now you are a big boy, aren't you?" This little six-year-old didn't know yet how much homework would affect his life for the next twelve years and even far beyond. And yet, by asking this question on his very first day of school, he showed a remarkable understanding of what was going to be important to him from now on.

For children at this age, there is only one world, their world. School life and home life are not yet separate entities. I looked at my students' parents, some shy, some eager, but all determined that their children should do well in school. One of the parents stepped forward with a somewhat reluctant child following. She pointed at the child and said, "I want him to do better in school than I did; he is very smart, you will see, I don't want him to mess up."

Here we were, lining up for our first day of school, with all of the children definitely slated for success. So where do we go wrong in our schools? I looked at the eager parents, who looked so young to me, especially now that I was over fifty, and oh so vulnerable in their hopefulness for their children.

I had just spent the summer with ten sixteen- to eighteen-year-olds from a troubled neighborhood of Newark, New Jersey. We had lived together for five weeks in the backwoods of the Shenandoah National Park, constructing and maintaining hiking trails. I got to know these young people, their strengths, their troubles, and the emotional pain they already had suffered in their short lives. I did not want to send these young people back into the troubled streets of Newark at the end of the summer.

Standing in front of my new class of first graders with their parents looking on, I thought about those Newark kids and asked myself what they would want me to do for them, if they were themselves their own parents. I thought that they would want me to be their teacher too, perhaps the teacher they never had, and to let them in on the secret of how to be a good teacher and to show them how to help their children succeed in school. The idea of inviting the parents and their children into the classroom for one afternoon each week suddenly popped into my mind.

I presented the idea to the principal and she immediately was very supportive. The parents could bring all their children, not only the ones that attended my class. On those afternoons, we all would do the homework together. We would call it Parents' Club, implying in the name camaraderie and partnership.

Learning Together

I wrote a letter to all the parents inviting them to our Parents' Club and I talked with them about it when they dropped off or picked up their children. I also discussed issues about my students after school during our class meetings. "Yes, mommy can bring the baby. Yes, your big brother can come too." Or, "No, you can't come by yourself; one of your grownups has to come with you." This was a new idea and there were many questions.

At our first session, we had two parents and five children. The children were eager to show their parents around so they quickly felt at home in the classroom. The first graders and their grown-ups settled down at our small desks while I helped the older siblings find a place to do their work and the little ones a space to play. I tried to be helpful without being intrusive. To a child I might say, "Why don't you use our buttons or the little blocks to do your counting?" and then make a casual suggestion to the parent, "At home you might use beans or toothpicks. Let them use different objects so they don't think they can only do their math when they have school materials." The parents very much enjoyed sitting with their children. The first graders were pleased to have their grown-ups' attention while they were doing homework. By third or fourth grade, children should be able to do their homework on their own.

The parents seemed to appreciate that I was responsible for the discipline during club time. The children followed our class rules. They did their work, cleaned up after themselves, and were kind to each other.

Our sessions were from 3:00 to 5:00 p.m. We had snacks around 4:00, sometimes provided by the administration and sometimes by the parents.

During the second half of the session, I usually set up an art activity, often expanding on our classroom project of the week. For example, leaf rubbings in October, masks around Halloween, holiday decorations in December, and kites in March. During our club time, the siblings could use our art materials, class library, and computers for their own homework. At the end of the session, the parents could borrow books and learning materials to use with their children at home.

"Nice" Homework

The parents' after-school, as it was often referred to, also gave me a better understanding of the value of the homework process and how important it is to assign the right kind of homework at the proper time. According to the parents there is "nice" or "good" homework. Those are assignments that are engaging, interesting, and manageable in terms of skill and time requirements. Parents and students appreciate it if the students can do their homework well. Then there is the "what does she want now" homework. This question often implies a sense of defeat and a somewhat antagonistic relationship between school and family. And there is also the "another one of those" homework. Boring, just pages and pages of filling in blanks and solving computation problems.

I don't remember having parents who didn't want homework at all. Homework is the number one mode of communication between school and home, and a way for parents to know what's going on in school. Good homework has to be carefully planned and well communicated. Homework, by its nature, becomes part of the family life, and different families have different needs. To be aware of these needs and to be flexible is important when giving homework assignments.

City and Country Resources for Parents and Kids

In addition to our weekly after school sessions, I organized club trips for the weekends. Working parents, who could not join us during the week, often participated in these outings. Also, parents who only spend the weekends with their children had the opportunity to meet their child's teacher and fellow classmates, and become part of the child's school experience.

When I was a brand new immigrant in New York City, the parents of friends and classmates of my three-year-old son helped us to discover the city and its wonderful resources.

I didn't know then, that it was all right to take three-year-olds to the big museums, and even better, for very little money: "suggested price, give what you can but you have to give something." I would have never read the small print, I would have been quickly back out the door, mumbling, "We'll do it another time," embarrassed that I couldn't afford it.

We planned trips to the museums and to the Central Park Zoo, and in the winter, we went ice-skating together, getting group discounts and often helping each other out with admission fees. At one time, we were even able to get funding for a weekend trip. We stayed in a cabin by a beautiful lake in the Bear Mountains. We cooked our own food and went boating. The children ranged in age from a nine-month-old baby to high school teenagers. At the beginning of the trip I gave each of the children a bandanna. After having carefully picked their favorite color, they each wore their bandana in their own style. It helped us to see ourselves as a group, as "us" instead of "me and them."

I often made picture taking part of our events. Taking pictures is a way of celebrating and of sharing and remembering good times. So each of the children was given a disposable camera to document this very special experience.

A Special Club Member

A mother of a student in my class was babysitting for a first grader in another class and brought him with her to our sessions. The little boy had a port wine birthmark on his face. He was very shy and almost always held his face down. I wondered if there were any possible treatments. I consulted my dermatologist and I learned that NYU Hospital provided laser treatments for certain birthmarks. The babysitter and I approached the mother. She seemed both reluctant and thankful. She gave us permission to take Sean for a consultation. A delegation of parents and children from the Parents' Club went with Sean for his first visit to NYU. The hospital staff was very kind and supportive and they offered Sean treatments at half the usual rate. The treatments took place every three months. In between the treatments, I asked for donations from fellow teachers and friends. Somehow we got the money together for each treatment. By the third year of his treatments, his family was able to take care of the payments. The trips to the hospital were not always easy for Sean. He had to keep very still during the procedure and the laser surgery was somewhat painful. But, slowly, we could see a change. Not only was the birthmark fading but Sean exhibited a newfound confidence and improved academic performance.

Sometimes, just one or two families came to our activities. At other times, the room was overflowing with parents and children. On those occasions, one of the adults would take the babies and toddlers for a walk around the school or play with them in the hallway. Not surprisingly, some of those toddlers did well when it was their time to enter school. They had been school babies.

I never commented about "attendance"; the Parents' Club was not about numbers, but about my commitment to the parents, to be allies in the education of their children.

I conducted Parents' Clubs for many years. It definitely helped me to be a better teacher and it helped my students and their families to feel more comfortable and more at home in school.

What worked for these teachers? For Barbara, it was the math lab. For Elena, it was simple rules e.g., respect, fairness, no violence, and the consistency of activities, the teaching circles, partners of the day, kid of the day, the use of appropriate and acceptable language, and singing the good-bye song at dismissal. For Jackquelynn, it was parental involvement, the literacy lab, and an ongoing process of self-refection. For Ursula, it was the multiage classroom, the class rules, the community rituals, the parents' club, engaging homework, and the use of the city and country resources for parents.

The teaching strategies presented in this chapter are purely individual. No one can guarantee that their use will result in effective teaching, a notion that is complex and not always well understood. However, the variety of instructional strategies used suggests that teaching is ultimately autobiographical and is a process of evolution. It is through ongoing reflection that we can untangle our successes and failures. The art of good teaching takes time and constantly evolves. Littky and Grabelle (2004) write, "Education is a process by which you put teachers and learners in the best possible environment for them to do this together" (p. 16).

Chapter Five

The Cautionary Tales

A teacher's work takes place in three arenas: teaching, administration, and interaction (Savonmaki 2005). They have to interact with students, parents, school administrators, other teachers, and so on. These relationships constitute what Iannacone (1975) refers to as the micropolitics of education, concerned with the interaction and political ideologies of social systems of teachers, administrators and pupils within the school building. Each arena requires a particular set of skills and competencies.

When interacting with students, teachers encounter a host of issues: classroom discipline, individual needs, students' motivation, social class, poverty, etc. Their interactions with students are open to public scrutiny. Teachers work in a fishbowl. People's open inquiries into their lives can cause them to design "protectionist" and "lobbyist" strategies to stay afloat. Protectionist strategies counter the impact of threatening behavior of others, e.g., criticism, gossip, rejection, and sabotage. Lobbyist strategies, on the other hand, build support, persuasion, reciprocation from other teachers.

Working with parents, observes Blasé (1987), teachers develop a diplomatic political orientation toward students' parents. This orientation results from the tensions surrounding values-related discussions with students, students' performance, behavior and discipline, teachers' extracurricular involvement, and the teachers' personal lives. Under supportive principals, the interaction tends to be more rational and productive. Under unsupportive principals the opposite occurs.

In the administrative arena, teachers focus on initiatives and demands of the school administration. This is a more distant role from teaching. It is peripheral at best and its effect on everyday activities is indirect. Barbara, Elena, Jackquelynn, and Ursula have worked with several principals. Although principals vary with regard to their effectiveness, they tend to emphasize control over students, orderliness, and high academic performance. They carry their own pedagogical ideas and beliefs and would not hesitate to micromanage classroom instruction when they feel that a teacher does not deliver instruction accordingly. Many principals discourage instructional innovations and reward non-instructional activities such as record keeping and attendance at meetings.

Last but not least, teachers must interact with colleagues. Jarzabkowski (2003) defines this process as collegiality, that is, teachers' involvement with their peers on any level, be it intellectual, moral, political, social and/or emotional. Gordon (2001) argues that teachers need plenty of opportunities to get to know one another informally, if there is to be any hope for the development of a trusting, open, and affirmative environment, which he sees as necessary for mobilizing schools to be their best. It is through these social interactions that expressions of need and offers of support can be made. Only in a safe, trusting environment can teachers ask for support (Jarzabkowski, 2003).

Barbara, Elena, Jackquelynn, and Ursula had to navigate interactions with students, parents, colleagues, and school administrators, and they have one piece of advice to give us: Be careful!

BARBARA

Would I Want My Child in My School?

My teaching career was only at P.S. 145. I began as a student teacher from City College of New York in 1964. I always felt that the students, parents, and the community were like a family to me. I was very fortunate to have a positive relationship with my students and their families. In the sixties, the teaching profession was still regarded with respect. I was there to teach, not to judge my students because of their color or background. I was very happy to be a teacher and regarded P.S. 145 as a fine school located in a poor neighborhood. Many years later, my youngest daughter, Jane, entered P.S. 145. In order to be accepted in the G&T kindergarten program, Jane had to take a test just like all the other students. She began in Elena's kindergarten class and began each day with a loud greeting, "Hi, Elena, I'm here." She remained at P.S. 145 until the fourth grade.

However, there were some tense situations during the last year of her stay. This is when Jane first encountered racism from her peers. There were a group of boys in her class who called her "whitey." When she came home, she would cry because she couldn't understand why they called her such a racist name. The classroom teacher handled the situation in a wise manner. Jane dealt with the situation and I was proud of her. She learned that school is not only about academic learning but about getting along with people of different backgrounds and ethnic groups. The learning that occurred at P.S. 145 was just as good as any elementary school in Queens where we lived. The teachers were competent and they had high expectations from their students. Jane had a positive experience. She socialized with students of different cultures and races, learned the basics, and developed a great sense of humor and the motivation to learn. Every morning for five years, when we entered P.S. 145, I was no longer Mommy, but Mrs. Storck.

ELENA

Respect Raises Us above the Isms

So, where to begin about the isms? The web that is involved is intricate and complex. I will first try to sort out some of the intricacies of the groups that might be involved in the isms. These include the relationships among teachers, administrators, parents, and children.

One such configuration was my teacher family. It was made up of all the pedagogues of the building, but not the administration. The teacher family is truly like a traditional family. We live together, figuratively, in our home, the school, for more hours per day than we spend with our own families (excluding sleeping hours, that is). There are the crazy aunts and uncles and the miserable cousins, the wonderful and supportive sisters and brothers, and the beloved elders. Sometimes we love them all, well, never the abusive or destructive ones. Sometimes we bicker and cry and yell and avoid and disagree. And sometimes, luckily, we find a few that are just the best match who support us and nurture us and agree on the same philosophy of life. This last group is essential for a happy school life.

Administrations come and go. Principals and chancellors come and go. I survived at least fifteen chancellors during my thirty-five years. That's one every 2 or 3 years. This fact is further proof that it is really just the kids and the teachers that are necessary. We had the big boss regimes, the in-law of the mayor regime, the incompetent regime, the "I am going to fix it" regime. All failed, all were replaced. We also had the good guys under the good guy mayor. These chancellors might even have been educators; maybe they had spent a year in a classroom. Well, maybe one I remember. Sadly, one good guy died. Every single chancellor was a man leading a faculty of at least 60,000 pedagogues who were mostly women. What is wrong with that picture? It is the women who know what works and have known for years because they have been there every day, in and out of political upheavals at the mayor's office.

Trying to establish a relationship with a chancellor is not on the teachers' agenda but trying to forge one with a principal is. In thirty-five years, I worked with at least nine principals. The longest and the most accomplished among them lasted ten years. She was an excellent early childhood educator. She had spent many, many years in the classroom and then wore many other hats on her way to becoming principal. Not like these days in the corporate Department of Education where principals are licensed with very little experience in a classroom and then expect seasoned and accomplished teachers to suffer their idiotic and incompetent programs and directives that the teachers know will not work. Others were nice but retirement loomed. Some were megalomaniacs and tyrants. I closed my door and continued to smile and nod. But I learned early on that it is important to have a working relationship with a principal without losing your own integrity. After all, they are the bosses. Therefore, principals are also members of the school family. It is a balancing act. Sometimes, being a principal is a lonely place, one is a colleague but boss as well, and possible friend but supervisor. Principals should not take on the role of mother or father in the school family. When that happens, teachers tend to retreat into the very comfortable position of children or sheep and forget how to make decisions, which leads to surrendering the hard-won rights that many strikes and union advocacy provided.

So, in this cautionary tale, it comes down to this: if you have integrity and are doing a great teaching job, hold your head high and close your door (or leave it open) and do the right and compassionate thing.

Administrations come and go, kids and teachers remain.

One major ism that I did not ever encounter in thirty-five years of teaching was homophobia. But, that was not because I was not gay, because I am. Here is where my school families show their fabulous strengths. I worked for years to establish meaningful and respectful relationships with all of my school families. I was respectful, loving, and caring. I provided a strong educational and emotional environment for my students and their families and for those of my colleagues who were interested. Because of this, my beloveds, whether they were my students, their parents, my colleagues, my administrators, my food service workers, or any other circle, always quietly watched my back. Not once in thirty-five years did I ever hear a pejorative remark. I do believe that comments and slurs were swirling around but I felt there was a circle of love and protection surrounding me. I did not realize that this was happening until my twentieth year of teaching. I came to realize it after the birth of my daughter, whom my partner and I welcomed into the world with much joy.

And so did each one of my school families. Celebrations and gifts and best wishes came in abundance; curious questions by newcomers were quietly answered out of my earshot. My classroom door was decorated in a baby motif upon my return to work; announcements were placed over the time clock (reflecting the culture of the school for new babies). It was then that I realized that this circle of love and protection had always been around me, back to my earlier years and my first school in Harlem. Never a derogatory remark! My families always quietly had my back. What goes around comes around for sure. Respect begets respect and sometimes it happens in the subtlest of ways.

Cliques!

Beware of cliques; they are insidious and seductive. They keep colleagues divided. They are obviously not inclusive, and therefore not respectful.

In my teaching life, I was always a maverick, pretty weird, on the cutting-edge of pedagogy. Most people in the school community did not know what to do with me. I was a threat to many people's pedagogic belief systems. I liked to shake up the thinking, upset the status quo. I was a consummate advocate for the children. I lived an alternate lifestyle. In a nutshell, folks were afraid of me. I might rub off on them. I was new to the school (where I inevitably happily remained for seventeen years) that already had a well-established village system. I quickly earned respect as a motivating and caring teacher. In my first year there, I taught two of the senior teachers' daughters. They gave the stamp of approval to this new yet experienced teacher's innovative and successful if unconventional style.

But I was always something of a misfit. I did not play the existing political games. I challenged old practices, e.g., yelling at children, size order line walking, gender line walking, gender roles (we need two strong boys to help carry books), quiet in the hall, expanding the classroom into the corridor (after all, I was the original Open Corridor teacher).

Over the years, I gained much respect. Slowly, a small cadre of like-minded teachers recognized each other, a band of parents started to appreciate and understand my style. The circle of parents and families continues to grow farther and wider than the pedagogic community, to this day. I often hear from friends and colleagues in the school community how they bumped into someone on the street, store, or bus and after beginning to talk about their children, the talk would come around to "Hey, you know Elena too."

But, back to the cliques. Unfortunately, even though I was treated with kindness and respect, rarely, was I asked out to lunch with the "girls" on half days, the girls being any small group of teachers that regularly met together socially in or out of school. Then, there would be the many awkward moments over the years when I would walk into a neighborhood restaurant with a friend during an extended lunch time, only to come upon the girls, some of whom had already made excuses about where they were eating, or planned their rendezvous in whispers in the lobby before we were released for lunch. In Brooklyn and the Bronx, we call that "behind your back in front of your face." Often in these restaurant groups, there would be some teachers who sometimes ate with me alone or in smaller groups; they would have the pained look of oops, the sad smile of I'm sorry but I am a sheep.

Then there were times in the last two years when my partner who was teaching with us and was included in one of the groups would be invited to various lunches, after-school, and weekend events and I would not be included.

I was always a little too weird for them. I rocked the boat. I quietly hung with the "others," my gay "brother," my crunchy "sister," or my very politically out there friend, or alone, or with the strays who inevitably found me with their stories of failed romances, troubled teenagers, or health issues. There was a joke amongst my beloveds that there should be a sign above my door akin to Lucy in *Peanuts*, stating 'The Doctor is in."

So, cliques are bad. We try to create balanced and caring respectful class environments. Classmates do not have to like everyone but they do have to coexist every day for over six hours in a peaceful and cooperative dance of personalities. But it seems that sometimes our colleagues forget to transfer that to their adult community.

Cliques are bad, be kind.

Racism

I keep returning to the circles that are formed within the intricate relationships of a school family and village. I have always wondered what teaching would be like if it were only the group of children and the teacher without the encumbrances of supervisors and administration, building politics, interpersonal machinations, and parents.

It is a juggling act. All these groups come with their baggage of life, their opinions, viewpoints, and prejudices, and we as teachers are supposed to magically create a happy and peaceful environment that is conducive to learning. And, this is supposed to also magically happen on the first day of school!

In the two schools of my teaching life, even though the ugly specter of racism has swirled around in my many circles, it was usually resolved in the way any homophobic issues were, i.e., by the circle of beloveds. It just was not tolerated, enabled, or given a voice. Some angry parents would make accusations of racism when it was too painful to address the problems of their own family structure or the educational needs of their children. But, yet again, I was blessed with colleagues, other parents, and administrators who consistently over the years would not engage in such accusations and would speak of my integrity and respect for the children. Issues were dealt with on their merit and then resolved and were not allowed to be complicated and obfuscated by irrationality and name calling.

I experienced only one major incident involving the nastiness of racism. Long ago in Harlem, after teaching successfully and happily in my first school for eighteen years, the winds of change were blowing, and after many years of corruption by district administrations, and as the Board of Education was bearing down to clean the district up, I had the opportunity to transfer to another district that was more welcoming to my progressive and modern teaching belief.

But, transferring in the NYC Board of Education, in the late 1980s, was not for the lighthearted. After teaching at that first school for so many years, I had a great reputation in the community and among the parents and children and many of my colleagues. I had started out as a very young, enthusiastic twenty-year-old teacher and was trying to transfer as a thirty-year-old senior and respected teacher. Pilot programs from CCNY with Lillian Weber and Columbia Teachers College with Lucy Caulkins had been started in my class-room. Scores of student teachers had passed through my door from Fordham University, CCNY, Teachers College, and Hunter College. I had done my job of passing on good teaching practices.

But, when it was time to get my transfer papers signed by the appropriate principal, district supervisors, and parent leaders, the doors started slamming. "We trained you" and "You owe us" were repeatedly screamed at me. But mostly it was the silent treatment. The same folks who had sung my praises and rode on the tail of my success were now my foes. My success had been their success and as their world was crumbling due to their bad choices and practices, they did not want to let go of people whom they could point to as examples of their success, as they were falling into the abyss of disgrace.

Administrators who had been my teaching colleagues and friends years earlier, were now those who were denying my professional growth. The logic was counterproductive. If I were made to stay, anger and betrayal would have tainted my abilities.

The response that I had hoped for would have been, "Thanks, Elena, for all your work for so many years for all of our children. Good luck." And with a simple stroke of a pen by my school principal, the transfer would have been approved. I was made to endure long waits at appointments with the district superintendent, the assistant district superintendent, and the district parent official, all of whom had been my colleagues and ardent supporters in prior years.

But this is all just the background for the most painful racism that I experienced. And that, sadly, was at the hands of my African-American friends who were my teaching colleagues. Time is of the essence when it comes to transfers in the NYC Board of Education. As the days passed and the hours and seconds ticked closer to the late spring deadlines for filing my transfer papers, after being stonewalled by my supervisors for weeks, I was anxious and frantic. I sought the advice and assistance of my teacher friends. Maybe they could prevail upon our principal, administrators, and parent officials to approve the transfer. After all, we had been friends; we had celebrated our children's successes together, our marriages, etc. We had supported each other in sadness and illness. They had protected me; they had been the circle of friends that watched my back.

But, when I did ask for their help, the response unfortunately was, in turn, "No, I can't help you." Euphemism for "I have to stick with my people."

So, why are these reflections being included in this study of our teaching lives and our attempts to examine and explain how good teaching might be replicable? Did we decide to include it because it had given us so much pain over our collective 100 years of teaching and so we had to yet again vent the anger? I have wondered over the past months, how will exploring all the isms create a good teacher? I was stuck. Then, upon rereading the title of this piece, the light bulb went off. Respect Raises Us Above the Isms. Aha!

One of the key elements to my successful teaching journey had been the recurrence of the concept of respect. Telling the painful memories or the more heartening ones of enduring or rising above the isms will serve as yet another prophetic example to those that come after us as to how to avoid the damage and choose the high road.

How does respect transfer to effective, compassionate, and successful teaching practice? Respect for oneself and one's whole school family creates understanding, inner peace, and contentment. Happy, emotionally healthy, and peaceful individuals make nurturing and caring teachers.

Always take the high road.

JACKQUELYNN

Ableism and Assumptions

As I moved into the community of education, I began to let go a lot of assumptions I had about teaching, about teachers, children, and school. Only until you are in the hallowed halls do the layers begin to peel away. I assumed all teachers would be dedicated to their craft and approach it with enthusiasm. Many teachers maintain these attributes even after lengthy years of teaching. It is often the newer teachers who are often innovative and eager to meet the challenges before them. They enter with a sense of idealism. However, too many teachers seem to have stayed too long at the fair. Lessons were often lackluster, methodical, not creative or stimulating. Many teachers were not only ill prepared to teach a subject, they lacked the personal desire to prepare themselves. I remember trying to have a discussion with a teacher about reading a particular book the grade was using for instruction. The reply from her was that she only read the synopsis. She said she couldn't be bothered spending the time reading the whole story. This "reading" consisted of about ten pages. As I observed her over a period of years, I noticed her room never seemed to reflect the learning that was taking place in her classroom. Her comment was that she did not like a lot of clutter in the room. She constantly complained about how her students were not motivated. She felt she taught the "basics" and that students did not need to waste time on "frills." In other words, no innovative lessons were attempted. Trips were not taken, unless made mandatory by the administration. What a sad class it was!

I found that the teachers that I was drawn to were those whose enthusiasm for teaching was infectious. I believe once a teacher loses enthusiasm for his or her craft the danger of complacency arises. To be an effective teacher means putting in a lot of outside hours, polishing the craft, and finding new ways to relay the information to students.

There were always teachers that set the bar of excellence extremely high. They were creative in their lessons, had enthusiastic personalities, and were organized in their tasks. They exuded extreme professionalism and warmth with their charges. Bulletin boards and classrooms reflected the learning taking place in the classroom. I have been witness to classrooms where stores were created to stimulate real experiences when teaching the concept of money. Life-sized body tracings were decorated and used for measurement. Original stories were encased in handmade books. Well-attended book signings for the "authors" were held. Good teachers are often those who are willing to share the teaching experiences that worked well in their classroom.

Make no assumptions about the children you teach. At the beginning of the year, you assume the child is prepared for his or her new grade. You have met the very dedicated and enthusiastic parent who gives the answers you are expecting. As the term moves on, you find the parents are not as dedicated as you initially thought, for many various reasons. The child is a living entity and lives in a world that is full of motion. Circumstances at home change. Family dynamics may change. All of this will affect the child in your classroom and how they learn at any given time. You assume every child comes from a loving home, with the basics: food, shelter, clothing. However, poor work may be the reflection of a family or child in crisis. The teacher may be the last to find out. My experience about one such family crisis revealed itself after having a conversation with a parent. Two hours later a social worker came to collect the children from school because the mother had just attempted suicide. Parents die and children often become seriously ill.

Crises that affect learning come when one least expects them. On Tuesday, September 11, 2001, we had just settled in for our morning lessons. Fortunately, I had moved with my old second grade into third grade. As a result, I had mostly the same children. I already knew 97 percent of the parents and the blue emergency cards had been returned as well. Despite the crisis and personal tragedies, two days later the children were back and education had to continue. There was the assumption that we would move back to normalcy. As I think back, there was no normalcy for the children, or for myself. But we were all able to move forward as best we could.

Another assumption is that administration will or will not be supportive. One can only hope to obtain support in this area. I had been fortunate to work with administrators who were wholeheartedly supportive. I also worked with administrators who needed personality transplants. Administrators who allow teachers some flexibility, those administrators that you can bring suggestions to for the good of the school, those administrators who have not lost their humanity are administrators who are the most desirable. Sadly, there are too few of them.

Racism

A wise woman once told me that racism is like a rock. We all possess elements of it. Observing the rock from a comfortable distance will not reveal anything. However, a slight scratch or abrasion will reveal the ugliness. Often, one has to drill down into the core of the stone for the revelation.

Does racism exist in our schools? I believe so. In reflection, I saw many layers of racism. One has to wonder why in a district that was so large there were so few minorities represented at the administrative and staff development levels. At times, it seemed instead of the old boys' club, it became an old white girls' club.

While listening to my fellow coauthors, I often felt how different the issue of race was for me. I don't know if they even realized that I too was suffering from racism.

Teachers, like other humans, bring with them their own personal baggage and their own prejudices to the workplace. Unfortunately, not only do they alienate themselves from coworkers, but this was also often passed down to their students, affecting their self-esteem and the ability to dream of a positive future. I have heard such chilling remarks that it would make me wonder why this person was even in the education field. Coming from a specific racial group or cultural group does not define a child's ability nor does it project his or her future. One frequently wonders why students, upon reaching middle school or high school, have so little motivation. If you feed a child a constant diet of statements of inferiority, the only result can be one of disillusion and lack of self-confidence. I recall having teachers express their disgust, calling minority children "animals" because they had poor class management skills. Recently, I took a teacher to task because of this very statement. I have overheard teachers in groups making statements that they were not going to break their necks teaching "these" kids who were only going to grow up to be drug addicts or dealers.

Teaching is the one single occupation that has far-reaching effects on a child. I can recall very vividly when a racial comment was made about a child when I was in the fifth grade. Even at nine years old, I got this sickening feeling in my stomach as I watched this child being humiliated in front of the class. It is even more painful when it is the adult who brutalizes a child in this manner. A child cannot defend himself or herself and may not even know why there is such hatred.

Sometimes, the racism comes from within your own group. As an African-American teacher, I have heard many parents express their disappointment at having one of their own as their child's teacher. Maybe they thought I was unprepared, mediocre, and lacking in knowledge. Or maybe they just believed the stereotypes that exist. Many parents compared what the other teachers were doing, until they found out that the children in my class were further ahead in skills, experiences, and learning. I recall an incident with a child who very angrily expressed to me the words of his grandmother. He said, "Our people are always hardest on our own." Hispanic parents were often hesitant as well. It seemed as if I spent the first quarter of every term winning over parents and assuring them that I was qualified, probably more qualified to teach their child than many others. It was unfair that many white teachers did not receive this same kind of scrutiny. As I look back at the ratio of minority teachers to minority students, it was an unequal balance. There is a need for more role models of every race and gender in the school system.

Having been educated in NYC schools and colleges, I did not have an African-American teacher until I went to college. And when I did, it was a bonding and rewarding experience to have such positive role models.

Black teachers face a peculiar hindrance, one that I have frequently encountered from peers i.e., not being Black enough to teach our children. Some black teachers were often vocally hostile, as if they were the anointed rulers of the Black culture. It is an ignorance I found hard to tolerate. However, there are always exceptions to the rule and there were always like-minded teachers of all ethnic groups with whom to coexist.

To deny that racism exists in the schools is to deny it exists in the United States. The schools are but a microscopic view of the society we live in today.

URSULA

Diversity Training

When I started teaching for the Board of Education in 1984, I was required to take a course in cultural diversity. The course was conducted after school in a classroom at a public school in upper Manhattan. Queens College provided the credits. All the students in my course were new teachers in District 5.

On the one hand, and considering the New York City student population, it seemed a good idea to sensitize new teachers to the diverse cultural backgrounds of their students. It was strange that a district with very little diversity among its students and staff would focus on diversity training.

During our first session in this required course, I made the unfortunate comment that people of different backgrounds should be tolerant of each other. "To tolerate others," the teacher replied emphatically, "was just another way of being racist." Everybody in the room seemed to agree with the teacher. I was stunned! I felt attacked and singled out as the only white teacher in the classroom. I made a note to myself to check the definition of tolerance. Perhaps the teacher had a point, tolerating somebody certainly entails an attitude of supremacy and I could see why our young black teacher would not want to be tolerated but respected.

On the other hand, tolerance is considered, by most, a noble attitude. The Southern Poverty Law Center even sponsors a program called "Teach Tolerance."

Was this just a matter of language, a matter of a misunderstanding? Racial interaction in this country is almost always a high-stakes game. There is no room for even a small mistake or misunderstanding. Like in extreme skiing or motorcycle racing, one mistake and it's all over. For the rest of the course, I sat quietly at my desk, trying to be invisible, trying to blend in. Looking back, it seems to me that I probably overreacted. To be the only white person in the room made me feel very vulnerable. I even thought that perhaps it was justifiable for the teacher and the class to be suspicious of and guarded against possible racist behavior on my part. As a mother of two racially mixed children, I too had witnessed and guarded against biases expressed toward them.

For my term paper, I chose to write about Native Americans. Under the circumstances, I considered it a safe topic.

I could have chosen to write about the civil rights movement, perhaps about voter registration in the South since I had some firsthand experience there. Or, I could have written about the Meredith March, now renamed The March against Fear, since I had participated in it. I still remember some of the songs that helped us to keep up our courage and our feet moving. "We are, we are not afraid" or "I ain't gonna let nobody turn me round" and "Oh governor Gartin you can't jail us all, oh governor Gartin segregation's got to fall." I remember this particular song so well because when we finally marched on the Capital in Jackson, Mississippi, it was surrounded by a large circle of National Guards, guns at the ready. It all of a sudden occurred to me that, indeed, we all could be detained and that quite possibly preparations had been made.

It was also on this march that I heard the Black Power chant and saw the Black Panther emblem for the first time. At first, I did not quite know how to respond. Shout along "We want the black, black power"? Raise my fist? Yet, somehow I was glad that somebody was shouting it. The tension, the almost palpable hate of the spectators, the car driven by a group of young white men that only barely missed killing us, the terrible heat, the blistered feet, not being able to step out of the marching column to use a bathroom for hours, made me feel so powerless. Hearing the cry for Black Power under these circumstances made us all walk a little taller.

Twenty years later, I found myself undergoing diversity training in a class taught by a black instructor and attended by almost all black teachers. Progress indeed. But I did not share my story. I did not want to take the risk of having it invalidated. The irony of it all!

Teaching Assignment Uptown

The Board of Education assigned me to School District 5 in Central Harlem. I interpreted my assignment to an almost all-black neighborhood as an attempt by the Board of Education to integrate, if not the students, at least the teachers.

Every morning, I took the bus from my home in District 3 up Eighth Ave to 132nd Street. Usually, the bus was crowded with people returning from their night shifts downtown, or with people like me, teachers and social workers going to work in Harlem. Once we reached 110th St., the passengers were almost all black and the mood on the bus changed. It became more relaxed, more neighborly. Greetings and inquiries about family members and shared acquaintances were exchanged among the passengers. The bus driver too became an uptown community member. Passengers boarding or getting off the bus engaged in friendly conversation. Comments like "Didn't see you on the four o'clock bus yesterday" or "Missed you last week, I hope you weren't sick" were not uncommon. Everybody seemed to know each other.

At first, I was almost uncomfortably conscious being white. But I was never mistreated. At times, people made a special effort to make me feel welcome in their neighborhood. After a while, I didn't think about it anymore and like many of the other passengers, I became one of the regulars.

This was more than twenty years ago, and at that time Harlem had not experienced any kind of rejuvenation, let alone gentrification. It looked rather dismal. There was a saying that if you wanted to make a movie about Germany after the world war, you just went to Harlem and you had your perfect backdrop. Sometimes it was difficult to keep up your spirits in such dismal surroundings of boarded-up houses and potholed streets. On one of the empty lots, a basketball net was erected on a gigantic pole. The pole was almost as tall as the four-story building next to it. Observing it daily from my bus window, I used to wonder what the message of this four-story-high basketball net was supposed to mean. "Try to achieve the impossible!" "Reach high!" or "Nothing is impossible!" To me it became the symbol of oppression, a basket set so high that nobody could score.

After my twenty-minute ride to school, I felt that I was in a different world. I could have used some of the cultural adjustment training that I received later as a Peace Corps Volunteer in Uganda. I hope not to offend anybody by making this comparison. I think it is important to acknowledge and talk about what it feels like to be in the position of representing "them"; of being a very visible minority. In intercultural or interracial situations, even little things like a smile, a gesture, the way you dress, your hair style, or the way you greet others are easily misinterpreted. The solution for me then, and later in Uganda, was not to be extra self-conscious but to be myself and at times have a good laugh about the precariousness of human relationships and, in particular, interracial or intercultural relationships.

Inequalities

After six years of teaching in Harlem, I transferred to my neighborhood public school. I immediately noticed that my new school had a lot more supplies than my old school. Uptown, the shelves in the school's supply room had been conspicuously empty. At the beginning of each school year, we were given a few pieces of chalk and some crayon boxes along with a small stack of paper. "Sorry, that's all we have," I was told. In disbelief, I asked, "Will there be more supplies later?" "We're supposed to get more but you never know," was the usual answer.

At my new school in District 3, reams of paper in many colors were stacked high on the shelves along with art materials and chart paper. I was given a whole box of crayons for each child and I could take as many chalk boxes as I wanted. I had to take a few trips to the supply room in order to carry all my materials to the classroom and I could request additional materials all year long. What injustice! In Harlem, it was a few crayons per child, and here each child got a whole box. But, crayons are perhaps not the most important item on the list of educational supplies. Sad to say, it was pretty much the same thing with everything else, textbooks, science materials, math manipulatives, paper towels, rulers, scissors, you name it.

Teachers' Choice implemented with the support of the teachers' union, the United Federation of Teachers, did remedy to some extend the shortage and uneven distribution of classroom supplies. Eventually, it evolved into a program where each teacher was given a certain amount of money each year to purchase materials for the classroom.

My new school in District 3 also offered many enrichment programs as part of the school curriculum, Orff classes at the local music school, recorder and clarinet instructions, art appreciation classes conducted by the Museum of Modern Art, and participation in educational programs in Central Park, to name a few. Both the school and the district administration constantly sought out grants and free programs to enrich the students' education.

At P.S.145 I also noticed a marked difference in the free lunches served to the children. Uptown, the portions were very small, and if children asked for more they were often rebutted by an unfriendly response. At P.S.145, the portions were generous, the children could ask for seconds, and the kitchen staff was friendly and approachable. Uptown, I had often seen kitchen staff carry out big bags, as if just coming from the supermarket, yet there was no supermarket in the area. I couldn't help but think that perhaps the kitchen staff took home some of the food.

Every so often, there were stories in the news about corruption in District 5. I remember one where a brand new grand piano had been purchased for a school but was delivered to the private home of a district administrator. Similar stories also surfaced about a school district in the South Bronx. It appeared that districts in poor neighborhoods had more incidents of corruption. Consistent and fair law enforcement often seemed lacking in so-called minority and poor neighborhoods.

Implications for Teaching: School and Classroom Etiquette

Young children live in the moment and have not yet learned to be prejudiced. But this is also the time when they start forming their opinions about the world around them. When it comes to social values, we mostly teach by the way we conduct ourselves. We can teach a beautiful lesson on racial equality but it is the classroom and school environment that will have the bigger impact. To quote the old saying, "Actions speak louder than words."

Within all schools and classrooms, there should be zero tolerance for any kind of derogative language regarding individuals or groups of people.

In the event that a child makes an inappropriate comment, the teacher should say in a matter of fact way, "That's not acceptable, we don't say that," and suggest an alternative. It is important not to get preachy or jump on a "soap box" in response to a racially or culturally inappropriate remark by a child. On the other hand, teachers who make inappropriate remarks should be fired.

Our acceptance of different lifestyles, cultures, and religions should be reflected in our school and classroom environment and in the school curriculum.

Class and school libraries should be well stocked with books about other cultures and religions. Within the last twenty years, there has been an explosion of children's books about different cultures, religions, and the diversity of our families.

Class trips are another way to explore different cultures and their manifestations in our country and neighborhoods. Many New York school children, including my now forty-one-year-old son, have learned how to eat with chopsticks on a class trip to Chinatown.

Songs, games, and holidays are a splendid way to celebrate other cultures and learn about them.

"Yes We Can!"

On November 4, 2008, Barack Obama was elected and became our first black president. As a nation, we are making progress on racial matters.

The narratives I've discussed bring up a host of issues: the relationship between teachers, administrators, students, and parents, identity politics, racism, teaching practices, inequalities, prejudice, integrity, celebration, inclusion, and exclusion to name some. Schools are microcosms of society. Whatever takes place in society at large also finds its expression in school. However, being in school gives one the opportunity to share, partake, confront, and serve. The reality of a teacher's work is that you have to be careful. There is never a dull moment.

Chapter Six

Becoming a Competent Teacher

When we began to discuss the subject of teacher competency, Jackquelynn reminded us that Rome was not built in one day. For several sessions, the group struggled with the question: what does it mean to become a competent teacher?

Etymologically, the word "competent" comes from the Latin verb *competere* which means to agree, to meet, to be fit, to be capable, to be proficient. Proficiency involves having adequate skills, knowledge, and experience for some purpose. Research on teaching, with few exceptions, has been conducted by researchers interested in teaching rather than by teachers interested in research. What teachers say is important to effective teaching and what researchers have studied and think often differ. Therefore, what is known is not always of great use to teachers (Reynolds, 2008).

In addition to the previous authors we have discussed on the subject of teacher's competency, the work of Roel J. Heinstra (2006) sheds additional light on the topic. Heinstra comments that a teacher plays four roles when teaching: (1) interpersonal, (2) pedagogic, (3) subject matter-related (content) and methodology-related, and (4) organizational. In addition to the aforementioned roles, a teacher must be sensitive to colleagues, to contexts (environment), and to oneself.

Heinstra's insights are worth revisiting. Interpersonal competency amounts to good management. An interpersonally competent teacher creates a friendly and cooperative atmosphere and promotes open communication. The teacher encourages children to be independent, and works to reach a balance between correcting and stimulating, confronting and reconciling, leading the way and following, directing and accompanying.

Pedagogical competency corresponds to a teacher's knowledge and skills that enable him or her to create a safe learning environment in which students can develop into independent and responsible individuals. The teacher ensures that the children know that they belong to a community that values and respects them and where personal initiative and self-discovery are encouraged.

Competency in subject and methodology represents a mastery of the content and the pedagogy. It is the ability to teach a subject taking into account individual learning differences among students and reflecting on the process. A teacher who achieves this level of competency helps students become familiar with their cultural baggage, a self-awareness that they need to function in society.

An organizationally competent teacher ensures that his students work in an orderly and task-oriented environment. Such a teacher insists that the students know what they can expect and how much freedom they have for personal initiatives and know what they have to (or can) do, how and why they have to (or can) do this.

In addition to the above competencies, a teacher must be sensitive to colleagues, to contexts, and to oneself. Competency with regard to the interaction with colleagues means the ability to communicate and cooperate with colleagues, to be a constructive participant in meetings and other forms of school consultation, and to participate in other activities needed for a well-functioning school, and to support its development and improvement. Although these standards are valid for most teachers, some areas of difference exist among primary school, middle school, and secondary school teachers.

Competency with context or environment amounts to good communication with parents or caregivers, and with any other educational institutions the child is involved with. The teacher has sufficient knowledge and skills to cooperate with people and institutions involved with the care of the students and his or her school.

Competency with oneself equals self-reflection, a process during which the teacher makes explicit and develops his or her views concerning the teaching profession and the teacher's own teaching skills. Such a teacher keeps up to date on professional activities and works to improve them. The teacher has a good perception of his or her personal competencies, strengths and shortcomings, systematically works on self-development, in tune with the policy of the school, and uses opportunities the school offers for further development.

The following narratives provide concrete examples of self-reflection, interpersonal skills, interactions with colleagues and school administrators, knowledge of the subject matter, and pedagogical and organizational skills. It took all these skills to build Rome.

ELENA

It's the five-year-rule (or sometimes the seven-year–rule) that no one ever told me about when I began teaching. I completed an excellent and rigorous teacher training course at a small university in the suburbs of New York City. It was the 1960s, I was full of bravado, and I was going to save the elementary school children of the inner city. I was fearless and had a great passion for children and teaching. I jumped right into substitute teaching in Manhattan and the Bronx and then into a full-time position. Teaching in middle-class suburbia was never in my plan.

My journey into the real world of teaching was delayed by my two years in the wonderful bubble of excellence, camaraderie, and abundant supply that the Open Corridor program provided. Then, I had my first class. It was a second grade. I was on my own with thirty kids, few supplies, not too many books, and a school environment that was a few steps above chaos. The environment in the lunchroom, recess yard, and dismissal was a disaster. The administration of the school was laissez-faire, do the best you can, contain the kids in the classroom, and don't bother us in the office.

So that is what I did. I didn't know any better. I taught my little school family using the tools and strategies that I had practiced in college. I diligently made sure we covered all the curricula areas. During lunchtime with some of my colleagues, I made language arts and math games using boxes that we would collect on weekends from now extinct hosiery stores. I made pocket charts, flashcards, and vocabulary cards with pictures from stacks and stacks of magazines from home. I covered music with a record player and Beatles' albums and with children's records from garage sales. Science had a lot to do with pet hamsters, planting beans, water play and, of course, the old dependable standby, the weather.

Time passed, I moved to first grade with forty-two kids, dabbled in fourth grade, and eventually landed in kindergarten. I did the best I could with the barest essentials provided, even though we were in one of the wealthiest cities in the world. Little by little, as the years passed, I started thinking more about how the kids learned. I watched their learning process. I listened to how they expressed their thoughts. I started noticing the patterns in the kids' learning. It was predictable in some areas of development; there was a rhythm of age-appropriate development. Somewhere along the way, my teaching style evolved from the top-down go, go, go approach that came from a feeling of knowing it all, I being all of twenty-something years old, to a more child-development-centered one. I would hear colleagues scold their students with rhetorical questions:"Don't you know any better?" I would answer in my head, "Actually, no, they don't or else they would not behave that way. It is our job to model and reinforce good behavior."

Because I was in a school and district that did not believe in or have money for (due to many reasons including corruption) staff development, I truly was isolated and unaware of the fact that much of the educational world was moving toward process and not product learning. I was coming to these conclusions on my own. My teaching was becoming richer and fuller with greater results and happier and more confident children. They were getting it because I was finally speaking to them and presenting information to them in a language that they could understand. It was an epiphany. After so many years, it is very difficult to pinpoint the exact moment, year or class. It was probably a developmental process for me and has no defining absolute moment. But there it was.

Once that clicked in place, my presentations to my many student teachers also changed. My delivery to colleagues who were in their first years had a more nurturing tone. I now knew about the five- or seven-year rule. I wish someone had told me about it. But, that is the problem with existing in a vacuum or on an island. Enlightenment takes longer.

I then began my two-part crusade. The first part was to make sure that I passed along to new and student teachers my discovery that maturing into a teacher takes at least five years. The first years are full of mistakes and experimentation, sickness and exhaustion, and lots of self-reflection and tears. It did not mean that they would not do a good job during those first years. It meant that they should take that time to find their own style and rhythm. They should be diligent, dedicated, and passionate, but not berating because it is impossible to know it all. One of my best principals told the story of how, in the 1960s, as a brand new teacher, she commuted between Manhattan and Staten Island on the ferry. She left very early every morning with her many teacher tote bags and wept during the entire ferry crossing. At 3:00 p.m., she would make the reverse trip with her tote bags full and she would weep again. This went on for weeks. She would ride the ferries with the same anonymous commuters every day, back and forth. Finally, someone asked a ferry worker if something should be done for this poor young woman who seemed to cry endlessly while riding the ferry. The ferry worker reported that it was okay. She was a first-year teacher. During the winter, when she had finally calmed down and had a bit of humor about her plight, the ferry worker told her about her concerned ferry riders.

Although I did not ride the ferry and I was not a mystery weeper, I would get up for work every morning and promise my bed that I would be back at 3:30 p.m. to curl up and get ready for the next day. Luckily, I was living at home, and my mother always called me down for supper. Many times, struggling student teachers and new teachers would find themselves hanging around in my classroom with my principal and me, and we would tell them our woeful tales. They were always surprised and also comforted.

Part two of my crusade became never letting what happened to me happen to other teachers, especially new ones or student teachers on the road to classes of their own. There is a philosophy that people should figure out the system by themselves because it will make them stronger and more resilient. I have observed that it makes people bitter and cranky. So I made it my job to make sure that new teachers knew how the system worked and never felt adrift or isolated. I felt that much of the mystery of a school's culture could be revealed with a bit of information. It is important to know how the attendance recording works, what fire drills look like, where the teachers' lounges and the restrooms are, what the procedure for lunchtime is. The list could go on and on. It is important to also make friends with the custodial staff and with the payroll secretary and to always remember that the principal is your supervisor and boss, even if you do close your door and do an excellent job, if not exactly by the rules and regulations.

Staff Development

Way back in the dark ages of the Board of Education in the 1960s, I had never heard of the concept of staff development. I have been trying to figure out why. I think it is because the people who were becoming teachers or who were already teachers came to the profession already with a solid background from their undergraduate studies in *education*. We truly studied, practiced, and trained in methods courses in all of the curriculum areas, reading, math, social studies, science, music, art, physical education. We endlessly practiced teaching in front of our peers as they pretended to be children. As early as sophomore year, we were required to observe classrooms for hours and hours in the local schools near the university. We were given small groups to plan for and work with. There was no photocopying then. We had to figure out the smelly xerograph machine.

My methods courses were rigorous. My professors did not play. Intricate lesson plans, reading and outlining piles of curriculum manuals, painstakingly practicing manuscript handwriting were all part of the assignments. This was in addition to my theoretical coursework and other academic pursuits like a minor in political science.

Then, there was student teaching. This was trial by fire, jump right in, five days a week, all day long, for six months while also still taking late afternoon courses. By the end, I was ready. I had my certificate. I knew I still wanted to teach. And I did. Again, trial by fire, I jumped right in to the NYC Board of Ed. There were no planned workshops or seminars, either in-house or elsewhere, with breakfast and lunch provided. Of course, the group of teachers I worked with in Open Corridor would meet amongst ourselves and discuss pedagogy and practice. It was probably around 1986 that I went to my first all-day workshop, Talents Unlimited. It was a new concept. I was really interested and inspired but also wondered where this had come from. Did the rest of the country know about workshops, was the Board of Education and District 5 just in the dark ages. Where did the money come from, why did we need this?

The Talents Unlimited workshop was also a milestone in my life because it was there that I met my dear friend and coauthor, Ursula. We were the only two who were not asleep—some were even snoring—around the huge conference table. We caught each other's eye, twinkled at each other, quietly laughed, and continued listening to the presentation. We probably chatted on the breaks, compared notes, met again at other workshops and inevitably worked in the same school. Life is a mystery.

The writing project by Lucy Caulkin from Teachers College appeared as an innovation for the teaching community. It piloted at my first school. I was hooked. It was brilliant. It worked. But, yet again, it had started in District 5 and was rejected as not appropriate for inner-city children. So, the workshops went on to the greener pastures of the middle-class districts downtown and became the cutting-edge of process and thinking.

From then on, the onslaught of what was now being called staff development was never ending. It sort of snuck up on me. Once there was none and now it was everywhere. Even the term "staff development" was new. For me, it was like a lot of the new vocabulary that was sneaking in, like when did roller blades become inline skates, not to mention all the high tech and computer terminology that was unintelligible.

So, why did all this happen? One of my theories is that the state of teacher education had become so watered down that teachers just out of college were unprepared. Gone were the days of rigorous teacher training. Anyone could get a teaching license in NYC with a bachelor's degree and the *promise* to take twelve credits in education in the near future. A whole generation of teachers who had degrees in studies other than education was out there unprepared and had to be developed on the job. The standards and requirements had become stricter in the ensuing years but were not rigorous enough.

Over the years, I had tens of student teachers. A few were great and passionate about education and children and went on to successful careers as educators and authors. But most, were mediocre. These included students from Columbia Teachers College, NYU, and Fordham. They or their parents spent lots of money, but the training was spotty at best. Excellent cooperating teachers were hard to find. Supervisors for the student teachers were often doctoral students who were more interested in their personal theses than in their charges.

For example, one of my very best student teachers, Meredith, was from Columbia Teachers College. She was presenting her very well-prepared final lesson for review by her supervisor. Her supervisor was a doctoral student and thought herself to be on the very fast track to becoming a professor. She had taught for a total of three years and considered herself an expert and quite accomplished.

Meredith's lesson was a comparison of the four different versions of the children's classic folktale *The Three Billy Goats Gruff* she had read to the children over the preceding three weeks. Meredith and the children compared the illustrations, the dialogue, the language, etc. They made a sophisticated yet age-appropriate chart together. It was a stellar lesson. Meredith was a confident, relaxed, and loving teacher. She was also a concerned graduate student who wanted the observation to be successful. I sat quietly off to one side so as not to distract the children. I was also observing so that I could comment informally to Meredith later in the day. I was also watching her supervisor who was, instead of focusing on the class, reading her own typewritten papers that were lying in her lap, which she had tried to surreptitiously hide by spreading her tote bags and other books around the small kindergarten table. The lesson ended and Meredith and her supervisor stepped into the hall for their post-observation conference. It took all of five minutes. Meredith came back into the room with a strange smile on her face. I asked her if her supervisor thought it went well. Meredith replied that she was sure she would get an A on the observation because when her supervisor asked her if she thought it was appropriate for the lesson to be about *virgins*, Meredith very calmly explained that it was really about *versions*. And, she had clearly stated that in the lesson plan that she had submitted to the supervisor the previous day for her to read. Well, after a lot of very quick posturing and sputtering, the supervisor pronounced that the lesson had been excellent and that she had thoroughly enjoyed it. So much for attentive teacher training and respect!

In spite of such experiences, Meredith went on to be a dedicated and passionate teacher. But she was that way before she got her degree.

For most, help with placement after graduation was nonexistent. Even the best met with disappointment in the real world and went on to careers outside public education. This was the situation at prestigious universities. One can only imagine what was happening in the next tier.

So, teacher training was a mess. On-the-job development was necessary because so many did not seem to know what they were doing. Then, I think, money reared its ugly head and corporate education schemes started trickling in. Fancy packaging of educational theories abounded. School districts bought into the frenzy. They changed about every two years, coincidentally about the same time as our revolving chancellors. We would just start implementing a new math program and then another one was purchased. Reading was just as bad. Whole language was in, and then it was out. Phonics was out and then it was in. Class libraries were bought and then discarded.

And so, we had poor teacher training, revolving door programs, and stop-gap staff development as a solution. Many longtime, well-trained teachers were moving into the staff development positions, which were less strenuous than a classroom, leaving the kids to the inexperienced.

I was a grade leader for many years because no one else would take it on. We had monthly grade meetings with the hope that we would discuss mutual projects and policy for kindergarten. I would present item after item on the agenda and but for one of the six, there would be silence and staring or sitting apart from the group even though we were arranged in a circle, or chatting and whispering while the meeting was in session. I invited principals and assistant principals to meetings to witness this phenomenon. Nothing could be done. In the last few years before retirement, I did not volunteer to be grade leader. We tried having a rotating schedule. No one would call the meeting or it would mysteriously be canceled. Administrators would ask for minutes, but of course there were never any. It became too much work for them to reprimand anyone. What a mess!

Young pup know-it-alls with less experience than could even be imagined were all of a sudden experts and became staff developers and later coaches. They were not fools though. They had no classroom responsibilities and, really, there was no way to track their performance because the burden of results always falls on the classroom teacher. One principal did have the kindness and sensitivity to excuse me from staff development. She would say, "Yes, you are on independent special assignment today."

But, in the late 1990s, those of us old dogs that were left in the classroom were lumped in with the inexperienced, the apathetic, and the complacent. It was very infantilizing and disrespectful. As in the greater society, the elders are not cherished. We were mandated to attend boring and inane sessions during supposed duty-free lunch, preps, and after-school. The hard-won contractual gains were crumbling before our eyes. It was infuriating and one of the final blows was when a young, supposed math expert conducted a lunchtime math workshop on how to use the calendar as a teaching tool. We had written that curriculum years ago. That was the end of my participation in staff development. I made myself unavailable and eventually they stopped trying to track me down.

It seemed to me, then, that there were multiple attempts at quick fixes of the system. There was no master plan, and the one thought that kept recurring to me was: What a mess!

JACKQUELYNN

Rome Was Not Built in a Day

During the process of writing this book, a lot of reflection was done. It was unexpectedly emotional, welcomingly satisfying and, at times, hilarious. Through it we returned to the question, "How did we get there?" I have been told I was a good teacher by students, parents, administrators, and peers. If I am, I did not do it by myself. I had help from many sources.

During my lunch hours or prep times, I walked the halls observing teachers, teaching styles, classrooms, and content, asking questions. It was on one of these walks to the kindergarten area that I met Elena. She was always welcoming and relaxed in a classroom of busy little people who seemed to possess a sense of self-assuredness that many of their peers in other classes lacked. I remember going into Ursula's room and seeing the blanket tents, oversized cardboard boxes, weaving looms, and the poetry. I looked forward to Barbara's visit to my classroom to demonstrate math. She always made herself available for my endless math questions. Maria demonstrated concrete math for the six-year-olds and Edwidge was an expert in classroom organization. I marveled at Linda, whose years of expertise as a paraprofessional in special education helped her handle the most difficult children, not only in her classroom but throughout the school, with quiet patience and an abundance of love. Chris had a gentleness that kept us all in awe, and Barbara W. created stimulating classrooms for the Gifted and Talented and then later created a challenging physical education program. Felice served as my unofficial mentor and put up with my unofficial observations of her class. Perhaps the single person I credit the most with helping me become a competent teacher is the staff developer assigned to our school, Jacqueline Morrison. Jackie, as we called her, provided much encouragement to new and also to experienced teachers. She came weekly with ideas, sat with us to make classroom materials and conducted workshops for teachers.

I learned years later that I am a lifelong learner. I enjoy the process of learning a new skill. For me, learning is an ongoing process. It does not end with a graduation or a certificate.

How did I get to the point where I felt I was doing a more than adequate job? It had taken many, many years. In the beginning, late at night, there was always questioning and reflection. How could I have done it better? Did I say the right things? Could I have used better examples? There was always the self-reflection.

Let no one tell you differently. The first years are hard! There is always self-doubt. "Is this the right job for me?"

It took me a whole year to figure out the teacher manuals for reading! Then, it took me another year to learn that I did not have to do all of the activities related to the lesson. My class could not possibly work through them all!

For the first few years, I gave up any meaningful personal life. Don't make that mistake. Teachers need to de-stress. The stress factor is not a myth. It is real. I laugh aloud when the public decries the two-month vacation. They do not have a clue of the endless paperwork and the responsibility for being the caretaker for twenty-plus children at a time. (It amazes me that somehow excuses are made for parents taking care of two or more children. Yet, no one ever considers how difficult it is to care for a classroom). Have no illusions, you *are* a caretaker. You will learn to care about your students. You become a family for ten months. If this is somehow offensive to you, please pack your bags and start walking away now!

I spent many personal hours (and let's not speak of the personal dollars spent and not reimbursed) looking for concrete examples, activities, models, etc. I integrated my curriculum as much as possible.

Slowly, but surely, I evolved. There was no conscious awareness of this evolution. It came slowly. The panic subsided and an air of assuredness took its place. However, I did not rest on my haunches. I continued to grow, learn, study, and reflect.

Rome was not built in a day. It was built with slow but steady patience and perseverance.

Staff Development or Is It?

I think when staff development is presented to teachers it is meant to be a positive way of imparting knowledge to the working teacher. Over the years, I've watched staff development of teachers change from exciting and enthusiastic and meaningful sessions to dictated, boring, and sometimes demeaning events.

At the beginning of my teaching career, I availed myself of staff development and workshops eagerly. They were informative and added tools that enhanced my teaching skills. On many occasions, they provided resources, samples, or ideas for teacher-created materials. There was always something that could be taken back to the classroom to be used immediately. Trainers were well versed in their particular subject. They knew their materials, had done their time in the classroom, and spoke with years of knowledge and experience. One of our district's best staff developer was a petite, effervescent woman, Jackie Morrison. Her role for me was more of a teacher-trainer. I credit her for giving me confidence and the encouragement to try new ideas.

The atmosphere was one of camaraderie. We felt free to speak up, exchange opinions, ask for help, etc. Often, staff development or workshops took place off-site (i.e., City Science at CCNY, at the district office, or in our own school).

I found the workshop topics often provided me with guidance in areas where I had less familiarity, specifically math and science. Frequently, we were paid for the two hours spent, including carfare. And better still, if we attended over a long period or during summer, we were paid a stipend.

While no one was forced to attend the trainings, I noticed early on that the same teachers would consistently attend. For me, personally, it was a learning experience.

In more recent years, the tone of staff development became one of oppression. Almost all staff training takes place in the school. Teachers are required to attend, even though they may already be an expert on the subject. The leaders were often not prepared, and had moved into the job through nepotism. Often, these were teachers who had tired of the classroom and had decided to move into the role of staff developer.

I think teachers today need a lot of 1:1 with good, experienced, enthusiastic teachers. I meet very few young teachers that will stay the test of time. They are paper-whipped and procedure bound. I don't think much thought has been give to developing the "teach" in teachers.

URSULA

Becoming a Competent Teacher

During my early teaching experiences, just being able to meet basic requirements was my primary concern. The daily demands seemed overwhelming. Teachers, especially in public schools, have endless record-keeping chores. Curriculum requirements and demands were not always accompanied by the necessary materials. I often had to scrounge, improvise, or come up with my own. And, of course, there were the children, so many of them and each one of them a very special person.

Bethesda Community School

It was in 1966, at Bethesda Community School near Washington DC., that I finally was able to become the teacher I always wanted to be. By that time I had become familiar with the needs of young children and I knew how to respond to those needs in the classroom. I had learned to find the right balance between providing active and quiet activities in the classroom, and when to switch from one to the other. I had become skilled at conversing with one student while still being aware of what the other thirty children were doing. I had developed those "eyes in the back of my head" and those ears that could hear each student in the classroom. At Bethesda Community School, I was able to take another big step toward becoming a master teacher. The school was well run. The class size was manageable. I now had twelve to sixteen students instead of sixty-five. I could focus on the individual children and get to know them really well. I started to reflect on my teaching in a much more thorough and analytical way.

The educational philosophy of the school was explained to me in simple terms as taking "the middle of the road." "Dear Ursula," the director of the school said. "We have done it the authoritarian way and we have let the children be in charge, but now we know that children need both, guidance and freedom." Classes were small; emphasis was on play and keeping things simple. An old orchard served as the schoolyard. There were rows of swings and plenty of tricycles for riding through the mud. Trees were for climbing. Adults were kind and understanding. In this comfortable and supportive setting, I was able to expand and deepen my understanding about children. I had ample opportunities to observe and interact with individual children and to discuss my observations with the caring, knowledgeable staff.

Six weeks into my stay at the school and still very limited in my English, I found myself in charge of a group of four-year-olds. I had been working as an assistant with another teacher when, unexpectedly, I was asked to fill in for one of the teachers, Ms. Bernice. Somewhat honored by the implied confidence but with butterflies in my stomach, I agreed. "The other teachers will help you and the children will know what to do," the director assured me.

Before starting her three-week leave, Ms. Bernice showed me around her classroom and explained in detail the children's daily routines.

Happily, I reported to the four-year-old room the next Monday morning. I knew how to greet the children, to help them hang up their coats, and to guide them into the activity centers. I smiled and nodded a lot, reassuring the children that I was there, taking good care of them.

Everything went well during center time. I kept the children busy, kept the room and materials organized, and stepped in before conflicts got out of control. I spoke softly and kindly as was the practice of the school, and the children responded well.

And then came clean-up time. I gave the usual warning, "Just a few more minutes," and shortly after, started the clean-up song. "It's time to put the toys away. . . ." So far so good; but four-year-olds need a lot of coaching during clean-up time. They looked expectantly at me. They needed specifics but sadly I lacked the vocabulary. What to do? I went up to the first item that needed putting away and I pointed at it saying, "What's that?" "Scissors," the children happily replied. And, with a big smile, I said, "Please put the scissors away," pointing to the shelf where they were supposed to go. I should have remembered this word from way back when I was in secondary school but the four-year-olds didn't know that and didn't care, they happily obliged. And again; "What's that?" followed by a "Please put the crayons away!" What's that?" "Please put the puzzle away," and so on. Those four-year-olds were the best English teachers I ever had. They didn't judge me for not knowing and they did not get tired of repeating a word or a phrase, no matter how often I asked.

After our morning snack of juice and crackers, we gathered for story time. I had carefully selected the book *The Cat in the Hat* by Dr. Seuss. It was one of the children's favorites and one of the two American children's books I had become familiar with. I was also familiar with *Curious George*. But *The Cat in the Hat* was easier for me to read aloud. It had lots of rhyming words and words that followed phonetic patterns.

The children were pleased with my choice. They happily followed the familiar rhymes and patiently corrected my pronunciation errors as I stumbled through the pages. For the next two weeks, we read *The Cat in the Hat* almost every day. The children loved it. By the end of the three weeks, I had mastered it, and we started on *Curious George*. "This is George . . ."

As promised by the director, the children knew what to do and, most of the time, went right along with the schedule. But one day, perhaps snow was in the air, they just couldn't settle down for our beloved story time. I urged, "Quiet please!" and "Please be quiet!" but the children kept talking and fidgeting. I remembered a phrase the children had used and thought I would give it a try. Proudly, with my most serious teacher's voice I said, "Shut up," and indeed, the result was absolute silence. "Well done," I thought to myself.

At this quiet moment, little Adrienne courteously raised her hand. I nodded for her to speak, and in a very friendly way she said, "Teacher, you don't say shut up, you say please be quiet." I politely thanked Adrienne for her help and I apologized to the children for having said the wrong thing. I promised myself that from then on I would always say, "Please be quiet." Adrienne had taught me a valuable lesson. In a matter-of-fact manner, she pointed out my misstep and offered an alternative. No big deal. This is exactly the right response to somebody's, anybody's misbehavior. Adrienne had very good role models in her teachers.

By the end of the three weeks, my English vocabulary had increased tremendously and my pronunciation had improved. I had been the recipient of good teaching practices and I had greatly benefited from it. Learning with these four-year-olds had been fun. They enjoyed teaching me. They never put me down for not knowing. They were always cheerful and patient. And, they never got angry with me for not knowing. They truly were partners in learning.

Mississippi Freedom School

In the summer of 1966, I joined the civil rights movement in Mississippi. Among other things, I sorted donations from kind people up in the northern states and I walked the picket lines in front of local department stores. I also had the opportunity to help out at a Freedom School. The first Freedom Schools were founded during reconstruction, after the American Civil War. Their goals, then, were to give former slaves the tools to exercise their new freedom. Now, a hundred years later, there was again a need for Freedom Schools. This time it came in the wake of desegregation and the demands of black people for equal rights. Some adults were writing their name for the first time. People also learned how to participate in the political process and how to register to vote.

At the Freedom School, I met a teacher from Australia who introduced me to the book *Teacher* by the New Zealand author Sylvia Ashton Warner. Even though the book was not written as a teaching guide, it influenced me greatly in my approach to teaching reading. The idea that the content should be meaningful to the student who is learning to read made a lot of sense to me.

At the Freedom School, I also learned not to use food items for art projects when people around you are barely scraping a meal together. The potatoes I had bought for making potato prints ended up in somebody's cooking pot. Since then, I have seldom used food items in the classroom other than for cooking and eating. This lesson learned also served me well as a Peace Corps Volunteer in Uganda.

P.S. 145

During my first year at P.S.145, I had a class of thirty-seven fourth graders and a coat closet made for twenty-five students. Luckily, the weather in New York is fairly mild at the beginning of the school year, and the students were wearing only sweaters or light jackets.

And then came the first cold autumn morning when the children arrived at school in their winter coats. It was impossible to find hooks for all them and also to close the closet doors with all the coats inside. It involved quite a bit of pushing and shoving. Whoever designed those closets certainly had no clue about kids and coats. I made a mental note, "Ask the maintenance staff to please replace those broken hooks." I then started the first lesson of the day.

At lunchtime, when the students were lining up to go downstairs, I casually mentioned, "Don't forget your coats." Then total chaos ensued! A rush to the coat closets, coats on the floor, chairs and children knocked over, somebody crying, and somebody's new coat dirty and another coat torn, and all of this in less than a minute! By the time we sorted it all out, we were late for lunch. "Ms. Foster, you are late, you know we have another lunch group coming in half an hour." I humbly said "So sorry." And now, feeling even more defeated and inadequate, I trudged back to my now empty but still somewhat disorganized classroom. I picked up a chair here and a pencil there as I worked my way toward my desk and toward my own lunch. It was only twelve o'clock and I was already so worn out, and there were still more than three hours to go.

The coat situation needed a plan beyond the replacement of the broken hooks. When the students came back from lunch, I told them to go straight to their chairs with their coats and then directed them, table by table, to the closet and to hang up their coats. At the end of the day, we did the same routine in reverse, so that the children who had put in their coats last, would get them first. After a few weeks, the students knew the routine, and closet monitors made sure that everything went smoothly.

But, the next morning, an angry mother waited for me in the yard. She was the mother of the child with the torn coat. "I want to talk to you, what kind of a teacher are you anyway when you can't even take care of the children's coats!" I apologized and I really sympathized with the mother. I told her what had happened the day before and that we were doing a lot better now with the coats. I offered to mend it. She said, "Never mind, I'll mend it myself, you do have a big class." She was no longer angry with me and we shook hands. The mother was absolutely right, how a teacher takes care of her students' coats is a reflection of how she cares about her students. The coats were easy. They can be identified, sorted and mended, or even replaced. Reading and math skills or the lack of them are a lot more difficult to identify, sort and mend. But, as with the coats, having a plan is important, having the children follow it and having them help each other do it right is as important as relating to the parents.

Being Self-Aware All the Time

A friend once explained to me that he thought first-year teachers were the best. A new teacher myself at the time, I was flattered by his remark but did not agree with him. I knew too well about my shortcomings in the classroom.

Yes, as a teacher fresh out of college, I was up to date on the latest methods, had lots of enthusiasm, was young and energetic, and was ready to take on the daily challenges in the classroom. Those definitely were good attributes for a beginning teacher. But they are not enough.

At Bethesda Community School, I became reflective about the choices I made as a teacher and how they affected my students. Living in a new culture and learning to think in a new language made me super aware of my surroundings. That, too, affected the way I looked at my teaching practices.

At the Freedom School in Mississippi, I learned how important it is for a teacher to identify with her students, to walk in their shoes or, as frequently was the case there, without shoes. This lesson learned served me well during my teaching career and during my Peace Corps tour in Uganda. I considered it a high compliment when one of the staff at the teachers' college where I worked in Uganda commented, "Kirabo (my Ugandan name), you don't separate yourself."

With the coat closet story from P.S. 145, I tried to demonstrate that a teacher always teaches and not just when she gives a math or reading lesson. One of the coat closet lessons was about caring, caring about each other and caring about our classroom environment. The other was about real-life problem solving. We had a problem. We looked for a solution, made a plan and tried it out. We reflected on whether it worked or not or whether it needed adjustments.

A competent teacher is intensely aware that she teaches every moment she spends with her students and knows how to make the most of it.

The Decline of Staff Development/Training

Even today, after being retired for four years, the word staff training still evokes strong and mainly negative feelings.

Starting with the physical environment, staff development was often conducted in school classrooms. Imagine thirty adult-sized bodies packed into a kindergarten room. High school teachers at least were able to sit on decent-sized chairs. Still, they had to cope with gum stuck under desks, lewd graffiti carved into the desks, and yesterday's spilled soda making everything sticky. I myself had this kind of high school desk experience in 1983, when I took my Board of Education licensing test at the Martin Luther King Jr. High School in Manhattan.

Also, through the years, special workshops for groups of selected teachers conducted during regular school hours sometimes took place at the district office. Elena and I made our first acquaintance at such a workshop.

We were attending workshops for teachers of Gifted and Talented classes in District 5. The offices of the district were located in a school that had been a private boys' school with tennis courts on the rooftop and a swimming pool in the basement. Now, part of the building was occupied by a District 5 middle school, and the remainder by various district offices. Our training was conducted in a lovely conference room that still held an echo of privilege and stateliness. All of us twenty-five teachers were seated around a very large, very beautiful wooden oval table. No sticky desks or splintery chairs here. What a treat!

We were attending a series of workshops titled Talent Unlimited. A special consulting firm from out of town had been hired to conduct the workshops. It was the first time I had attended workshops that were carried out by a professional trainer rather than by a Board of Education educator. I had questions and, yes, some objections to this approach of teacher training, but, wisely, I kept these to myself. The district obviously had spent a good deal of money on these workshops. Colorful posters depicting graphs that highlighted the benefits of this method were placed around the room. It all had a bit of a sales pitch to it.

Still, I enjoyed the workshops and definitely walked away with some new teaching ideas. The district did expect us to use this newly introduced teaching method in our classrooms, but we were given some leeway in when and how to implement it. Overall, it was a good experience.

When Elena and I met there, we could not know then that both of us would end up at P.S. 145. On my first day at P.S. 145, Elena approached me: "Remember me? We were the ones who did not go to sleep during the workshops at District 5." Memories of the oval table in that lovely conference room came back. Indeed, many of the teachers around the table had nodded off and were actually softly snoring during the workshops. And we didn't know then that we were birds of a feather, quietly grinning at each other over our sleeping colleagues. But I must admit the workshops were a bit boring. And teachers are always tired. Teaching is physically and emotionally such hard work.

After transferring to District 3, I found teacher training, in general, more useful and fun. Teachers attending the workshops seemed more actively involved in our sessions and definitely more outspoken. They would not have put up with boring workshops, and felt safe to voice their opinions.

District 3 had an amazing math co-coordinator at the time. I remember attending some of her workshops, mainly after school. Attendance might have been voluntary; we also might have received a stipend. Her workshops were always packed and everybody had a most exhilarating time. Her sessions were very hands-on. Teachers never fell asleep during her presentations and she practically had to throw us out at the end of the day. We always came away with many new teaching ideas and were usually given materials for our classrooms. Teachers who had attended her workshops would talk about them for days and exchange notes on what they had tried out in their classrooms and how it had worked.

I also fondly remember a weekend trip with the District 3 science coordinator to an environmental center in the Catskill Mountains. We slept in cabins, attended workshops during the day, and square danced to old-time fiddling in the evening. We explored the natural environment around us and learned about setting up hands-on science activities in our classrooms. We also had the opportunity to meet teachers from other schools within our district.

But most of my memories about teacher training are not so positive. Sometime in the mid-1990s, policies about teacher training seemed to change. Schools now seemed to be required to conduct workshops on very specific topics. This might have been related to the newly launched standards. Professional development started to feel more like obedience school. Teacher training no longer was about becoming a better teacher. It was mainly to disseminate information about education policies and their implementation.

What made the implementation of the standards so complicated was that they were not standards in a true sense. Instead, they were a compilation of skills and learning activities for each grade level. The activities or standards were carefully catalogued. Abbreviations of each standard had to be included in all lesson plans and attached to all of the students' work. Imagine ascribing a standard to each and every learning activity within any given school day and keeping a record of it. The very rigid application of the standards to all teaching activities was very frustrating because it was so counterintuitive to how children learn.

It was very difficult to get teachers enthusiastic about the standards. Teachers needed a lot of training to implement them. With emphasis on compliance, professional discourse was discouraged and considered a waste of time. Teachers quickly learned to sit quietly through those training sessions.

I do not want to end my reflections on teacher training on such a negative note, especially since I myself was a teacher trainer in Uganda. Fortunately, I could fall back on the good examples of training I had experienced during my early years in District 3. As in New York, teachers in Uganda were not always excited about attending. I tried to make our sessions fun and I tried to have materials for the teachers to take back to their classrooms. I once overheard a comment about my workshops: "People seem to have fun in her class." I took this as a compliment. When teachers attending workshops have a positive experience, it is easier for them to learn about new ideas and to remember them. They are also more inclined to try them out in their own classrooms as we did after those stupendous math workshops with our district coordinator.

The journey to becoming a competent teacher took multiple forms for each of these teachers. For Elena, it was a process of self-observation, self-discovery, and sharing her insights with colleagues and student teachers, to make sure that they would avoid some pitfalls. Jackquelynn, who came to teaching a bit later in her life, decided that one of the best ways to become a competent teacher was to observe good teachers, focus on self-reflection, and become a lifelong learner. She constantly sought excellence in teaching, spent hours in bookstores and on her computer in search of resources with which to work with her students. Barbara made mathematic "fun," a subject often disliked by many students. Acting as an assistant principal she made herself visible to the students, the teachers and the school staff always ready to provide guidance and assistance.

Sonia Nieto (2003) writes, "All good teachers whether they consciously carry out research or not are researchers in the broadest sense of the word. This is because good teachers are also learners, and they recognize that they need to keep learning throughout their careers if they are to improve. They probe their subject matter, constantly searching for material that will excite and motivate their students; they explore pedagogy to create a learning environment that is both rigorous and supportive; they talk with their colleagues about difficult situations. Above all, they value the intellectual work that is at the core of teaching" (p. 76).

Ursula honed her teaching skills by learning from her students who became her learning partners. She also learned from her interactions with the children's parents and also from her volunteer work with inner-city youth. Further, Ursula's convictions about education grew out of her years of activism in the civil rights movement. A growing awareness of the unequal treatment received by minorities and marginalized communities explains her deep commitment to teaching as a tool of change. There is a great deal to learn when one puts oneself in other people's shoes.

Becoming a competent teacher, therefore, is not an end, because neither learning nor teaching has an end. Good teaching is never completely mastered. It is ever changing, interesting, and challenging.

Chapter Seven

My Last Year Teaching

Elena retired on her fifty-fifth birthday taking advantage of the Tier I being offered by the NYC Teachers Retirement System.

Barbara accidentally slipped on ice and broke her ankle and decided to retire.

Ursula, who came back from Uganda, hoping to teach up to her sixty-fifth birthday, found out that everything had changed in school. As a veteran teacher, she had lived through a myriad of restructuring initiatives and reforms. She had enough of the arbitrary nature of the system, of those who did not see that schedules and superficial changes do not restructure schools. She took on her assignment as a kindergarten teacher and a few months later scheduled a pension consultation.

Jackquelynn witnessed many teachers retiring. She loved teaching but she knew it was time to close this chapter.

Everything comes to an end. Read on!

BARBARA

My Last Year at P.S. 145

My last year at 145 was a very unusual ending to a memorable and fulfilling teaching career. In September 2003, I began the school year like I did many others before, fixing up my office classroom, giving out math materials to my colleagues and, most of all, looking forward to another interesting and dynamic year trying to make mathematics a student-friendly subject that would prepare the students to use math in everyday activities.

Our school had been experiencing a few very tumultuous years following the retirement and premature death of one of our beloved principals. This era included four different administrations. Each principal had his or her own philosophy and ideas about what was needed to improve our school, even though the staff thought that our school had been working quite well. In February 2004, we were assigned a new principal and change was upon us again. However, my plan was to adapt to this new administration and forge ahead with my philosophy about teaching math!

On a cold, gray, icy winter morning, on February 4, 2004, instead of following our usual family plan, I decided to drive my daughter to Long Island College Hospital in Brooklyn where she was a fourth-year medical student assigned to a surgery rotation. She had to be in the operating room at 6 a.m. On that morning, instead of letting her leave at 4:00 a.m. to get to the hospital by train, I decided to drive her even though she didn't want me to. I arrived back home at 6:00 a.m., parked the car, stepped out of it and slipped on the ice. I lay on the sidewalk not being able to move. I screamed until a neighbor finally found me and the rest is history.

After a two-and-a-half-hour surgery to repair my broken ankle, and three months of physical therapy, I knew I couldn't return to my school. So, on May 17, 2004, I retired. It was such a disappointing way to leave a career that I loved so much. I considered my teaching career as a blessing. I thought of all the students that I had taught throughout my thirty-two-year career while I was recuperating for all those months. I just wish I could have been better prepared. It was so hard to retire when I was without a choice.

So, if you decide to be a teacher for your life's work, enjoy each day, be a good listener for your students, keep up with the last latest curriculum ideas and trends, be true to your teaching philosophy, and watch out for those icy patches along the road.

ELENA

The Last Year

Never ever, ever, ever, ever count down to your retirement!

I knew about not counting down way before I ever started thinking about retirement. I apply this to my life in general. Too many things can interrupt life. Then, the disappointments can take over. Long ago, I began adding "maybe" at the endings of plans I made with my children and family. Then, when things came to pass, they were even more wonderful because they actually happened and no one was disappointed by unfulfilled, absolute promises. It became my way of protecting my loved ones from the world.

How lucky I was, in retrospect, to have begun teaching at twenty years old, to have signed up for retirement during the short window when the jewel in the crown, Tier I, was being offered by the NYC Teachers Retirement System, to never have had to take any leave of absence for illness or child care and to have resisted taking the sabbaticals that were offered like carrots only to have to go back for two years after getting a taste of not working. So, as my fifty-fifth birthday started creeping up, I began to get serious about finding out about the mysterious and confusing process of retirement. Our union provided wonderful annual consultations for those planning to retire. They explained the multiple plans that one could choose the annuities, the never-ending and complicated paperwork, and its accompanying, unforgiving schedules that *must* be followed to the letter of the law. The Department of Education continued to have its head in the sand as we baby boomers started planning to retire. About 15,000 teachers retired in a three-year period from 2000 to 2003. That is more than the whole population of my small suburban town. The devastation of 9/11 increased that number as we faced the reality of embracing our blessings as soon as we could.

The union consultations were booked years in advance. Nervous and often neurotic NYC teachers swarmed the union and the parallel offices of the Teachers Retirement System at its infamous Worth Street building.

The bureaucracy does not make the retirement process easy either. But, little by little, I slogged through, first making the definite decision to retire in September 2003, a scant week after my fifty-fifth birthday in late August. Almost everything in the NYC retirement system revolves around birthdays and your first day of teaching. Sometimes, seniority went down to the exact day that you started. Of course, while still working, I had begun with the consultations and workshops and paperwork over a year before the exact date. Colleagues who also were planning to retire helped each other. Older friends who had gone before tried to help. Often, misinterpretation of information abounded.

One thing became clear. Because I was in Tier I, my pension would be enough for me to continue my lifestyle. How lucky I was! So, that was the bureaucracy.

But what about the teaching? I had to also get ready to not come to my classroom anymore. I had been on the school calendar since before I was born. My sister started kindergarten two weeks after I was born. September to June had been my rhythm forever.

Once I had made the decision to retire, I also made the decision to continue business as usual in my classroom up until the last second of the last day in June 2003. Why? Because the kids came first. They deserved excellence until the end. The little chairs in my kindergarten were definitely becoming a challenge. Sitting on the carpet was even tougher. So, I continued cleaning guinea pig cages, wiping noses, playing the piano, enduring the endless parade of bureaucrats touring to check on standards, facilitating literacy, writing and math workshops, eating yogurt for lunch (at least I wouldn't have to plan lunches for school anymore), attending endless staff development. I think it would be a good idea if after a certain point in their career, some teachers were exempted from being developed.

The months went by. I still never counted down. During every school year, it had been an activity in my class to count up and celebrate how many days we had been in school.

I began making plans for my retirement party. It turned out to be an "everybody's invited to my house for a huge potluck" party. A group of parents organized the kids from my first class at P.S. 145 to attend. They were in college. They came with their families. They were shy and grown. I was older and chubbier. Ursula, in the Peace Corps, sent a presentation from Uganda. People brought photos. We rented port-a-potties. Even though it was a rainy day, it turned out that great fun was had by all.

Then, it was the last day of school in June 2003. The last day was always a half-day. The kids went home at 11:30 a.m. We always had a closing circle time at the end of each day and then I sang the good-bye song with my children for the last time.

> "I don't want to say good-bye.
> I don't want this day to end.
> But we will be happy together tomorrow,
> Together tomorrow again."

Not this time.

JACKQUELYNN

The year prior to my retirement had been devastating. My mother became ill and finally passed away in May. I had been mulling over taking a sabbatical to nurse her, but life has a way of dictating its own path at times. On top of that, I suffered a horrible fall at school, weeks before closing. I was naturally depressed, but wise enough not to make a sudden decision regarding any life-altering changes. As I grieved my loss, I spent the summer healing from the physical and emotional pain I was suffering.

In September, I was looking forward to greeting my new students, and starting the new term. Upon returning to school, there was an absence of familiar faces and a replacement of newer ones. At our yearly back-to-school breakfast, someone remarked that the older teachers had to search for each other among so many newer faces. Years before, it was the newer teachers that stood out.

The class was a bright one. There were some behavior problems but generally it was a great class. They were eager to learn, with bright, inquiring minds.

But no class is perfect. Third grade is full of change. It is this grade where student growth is perceptible. Year after year, I watched students grow physically, emotionally. I watched them become more independent. They entered in the fall, still wearing their silken cocoons and emerged as graceful butterflies in the spring. A very peculiar paradox occurs. Some parents want to turn their eight-or-nine-year old loose. They think their children are displaying independence, and therefore do not need as much nurturing and supervision as before. I believe a lot of parents do not realize that gentle hand-holding needs to continue. I had an experience with one of my mothers who could not understand when the results of the Princeton math tests came in, that her child was consistently scoring low. Her foundation of math was poor and we had enrolled her in intervention classes and also provided her with tutoring. I provided material for her mother to work with at home, as well as lots of 1:1 in class. Her mother complained, she just did not understand. The child was almost nine, and at her age, her sisters and brothers did not have those problems. She wanted to know when she would be able to "turn her loose, so she could do her own thing."

Parents often discount a lot of the past conversations about potential problems students have in prior grades. However, third grade is the initial testing grade, and with No Child Left Behind, it became crucial to assess them early in the term to see if students would need intervention or if they were weak in comprehension or math skills. There is the initial frustration of having these talks with parents. It is at this grade that they begin to really listen to what is being said by the teacher. Many teachers have often sought to please parents by telling them what they want to hear and it makes it difficult to establish a "voice" with the present teacher.

The year progressed with endless walkthroughs and meetings, and it was as if the whole school community had become brittle, on edge, and humorless. More teachers kept their doors closed and generally kept to themselves. Certain teachers seemed to be administrative targets. Rooms were constantly being "redone" because they did not meet the Region's criteria. Blocks in the primary grades were removed and discarded on the street, and learning centers seemed not to exist at all. It was as if all the traditional historical child development theories had been tossed aside. There seemed to be this urge to cookie-cut each classroom. While there were teachers that were in need of assistance, so much wasted time was spent regurgitating demands from the Region. I became very disheartened by how administrators spoke and related to teachers. There seemed to be a lack of professionalism that came from the administrators.

However, one highlight from the last year was that eight of my young boys tested for the George Franklin Academy and five were accepted. However, only one student actually accepted the scholarship, attending in fourth grade.

By February, I began to think seriously about retiring. I did not feel I would be able to continue teaching in the creative, nurturing, and challenging style that I had developed over the years. I kept picturing what the next year would be like. I did not like what was on the forecast. While I had enjoyed teaching, I instinctively knew it was time to leave the party.

I had amassed a huge library and masses of materials for extracurricular activities. The majority of my classroom was left intact for the incoming teacher. However, my personal treasures were joyfully given away to the remaining innovative teachers on staff.

The year proved to be a melancholy one, tinged with sadness, anger, joy, and regret of leaving something I had so much passion about. There is a time and place for everything and perhaps this was the time to close this chapter.

URSULA

My Last Year of Teaching

My last year of teaching was my first year back after a two-year leave of absence to serve in Uganda as a Peace Corps Volunteer. In accordance with our union contract, I had the right to return to my previously held teaching position.

My Peace Corps experience had been absolutely amazing. I had learned so much about the world, about myself. I had learned a new language and I, especially, had learned to appreciate the many blessings in my life. I felt rejuvenated and I was excited about going back into the classroom. I had missed the daily interaction with the children. There was that special moment each morning when I picked up my class in the schoolyard and the children were so happy to see me. Twenty-five little faces looking at me wondering, "What are we going to do today?" A teacher is such an important person in the lives of children.

I had sent my assignment preferences to the school in early April. I hoped they would arrive safely and would be honored. In case the school had forgotten about my return, I hoped that this letter would be a reminder. To post the letter, I had taken a four-hour mini bus ride to Kampala. All the letters I had posted there, at Uganda's main post office, had arrived safely at their destination.

By the end of May, I was on my journey home. I flew from Entebbe to Athens and then traveled through Europe by train. While sightseeing in northern Greece, in the beautiful city of Thessaloniki, I happened upon an Internet café, and on the spur of the moment decided to go in and check my email. My dear friend and colleague Elena had emailed that, according to the school's reorganization sheet for September, I was to teach a kindergarten class. Rightfully, Elena had assumed that this would be the only way for me to find out before being actually back in school. She informed me that she was retiring and that I would inherit her classroom. "Don't worry," she wrote. "I will make sure that you will have plenty of materials. I won't let the other teachers take them. Everything will be packed away for you to use in the fall." Elena also let me know that there would be a new principal in the school in September. The current principal, who had been there for the last three years, was leaving. Her replacement had not been announced yet. "Enjoy your summer" and we'll see each other in the fall" was how her email ended.

I was quite relieved. I was expected back. And a kindergarten class, how much fun was that! At that time, I was planning to teach for another two or three years or perhaps even until my sixty-fifth birthday.

A week before school opened, I went to the school to introduce myself to the new principal. She was terribly busy at the time and I had to wait quite a while before I could see her. Finally, and amongst the hustle and bustle of the main office, I was able to introduce myself. Since I had not received an official notice, I wanted to check my assignment with the principal. I mentioned the kindergarten class and the room assignment. Her response somewhat surprised me, "Do you even know how to teach kindergarten?" I replied that I had taught kindergarten before, for quite a few years, and that I always enjoyed it. She continued, "It's all different now, you have to talk to her." She pointed to a woman who, as I found out later, was holding the newly established position of literacy coach. "She will tell you how to set up your room." By the way, the coach had never taught kindergarten. However, the new principal was right about everything being different, other than the children of course. But I was not too alarmed at the time, thinking, "Once the principal sees me working with the children, she will recognize that I am a good teacher."

But everything was indeed different now. For the first time in my forty years of teaching, I was actually being dictated to about how to teach a lesson down to the minute, and the seating arrangement of the students. During the first week of school, we attended many training sessions at various locations. At one of the training sessions, I noticed a group of teachers wearing bright blue T-shirts with the message "On the same page, at the same time, all of the time." I smiled at them and gave them a thumbs-up "good for you" and I pointed to their shirts. At least there were some teachers who had the guts to poke fun at the new Department of Education policies. The powers that be seemed to think that all children learn at the same rate and in the same way. But the teachers in the blue T-shirts did not smile back and their somber faces in response to my offbeat remark made me quickly melt back into the crowd. They really meant what their shirts proclaimed. This was definitely not the place I had left two years ago.

Still, I could not imagine that on the same page, at the same time, all of the time would be taken so literally. But that exactly seemed to be the trend. It was a simplistic way for administrators and supervisors to document their accountability. During the coming school year, during kindergarten grade meetings, we would make references to page numbers instead of to topics or teaching concepts. At one of these meetings, with both the principal and the literary coach in attendance, I found myself on the wrong page of the curriculum guide. Actually, I was on the right page according to the page number but it was the wrong page with regard to the content. After having been scolded and reprimanded for not paying attention, it turned out that I had last year's edition. "How come you have the wrong book?" I was reproached. "On the same page, at the same time, all of the time!" They were really serious about this.

By mid-November, building blocks and housekeeping areas were being removed from the kindergarten classrooms in compliance with a directive from Region 10. The children were supposed to learn, not play. Somehow, I managed to hold on to mine. Young children need to play and should have the right to play because this is how they learn about the world around them.

Three months into the school year, I scheduled a pension consultation. With the many sick days I had accumulated, I could retire on my sixty-second birthday in September and not go back to school after the summer vacation. Then and there, I decided that this was going to be my last year of teaching and that somehow I was going to make it through with my integrity as a teacher intact.

Somewhat surprisingly, six weeks before my retirement, I had a formal observation. During my post-conference, I was given some advice on seating arrangements for the children and on passing out markers. I never received the write-up for the observation but I let it slide. I knew of at least one teacher with a temporary teaching license who was not observed that year. She should have been a priority. Under the leadership of the newly renamed Department of Education, school administrators were under great pressure to give more U (unsatisfactory) ratings to teachers than in previous years. The rationale was, "How can so many of the teachers receive satisfactory ratings when the students perform so poorly." How easy it would have been to give a retiree a U rating.

For the rest of the school year, we enjoyed Mother Goose rhymes and played circle games. We painted and pasted. By February, most of the children were able to write "I love you" on their Valentine cards. The children learned to build intricate wooden block structures and to navigate them without knocking them down. Well, most of the time. When spring came, we moved many of our activities outdoors into our little kindergarten yard. Just by being outdoors, the children seemed to be more calm and happier. And, after all, the word "garden" inspires an image of being outdoors.

And so the last day approached. For the very last time, I picked up my students in the schoolyard, guided them through their learning activities and, at three o'clock, gathered them for dismissal. As usual we sang, "So long it's been good to know you, so long, it's been good to know. . . ." by Woody Guthrie, on our way out of the school.

At the end of this particular school year, eight teachers retired with a combined teaching experience of more than two hundred years. They would be replaced by twice as many teachers receiving one half the salary!

Chapter Eight

My First Year Out

Teachers' lives do not end with retirement. After working for so many years, retirement provides teachers with a respite when they can live their lives the way they always wanted to live but somehow missed out on, owing to their responsibilities and job pressure (Lee 2007).

However, retirement is not without its challenges. The new retiree must adjust to the no-schedule mode; not having to wake up early in the morning, commute, as in Elena's case from New Jersey to New York City, face a group of students at 7:30 a.m., attend professional development meetings, etc. Barbara soon discovered that she needed to use her teaching skills to re-teach her daughter all over again. Elena started with a glorious trip to Disneyworld with her two daughters. Back home, she began to learn about the culture of daytime activities in suburbia while also attending to her lovely aging mother. She also reflected on the teaching career that she loved, and felt at peace with her decision because she realized that had she stayed she would have slammed up against the corporate regime of the school.

Jackquelynn expressed the need for a physical and emotional adjustment for teachers after retirement. Her first year was a time of self-discovery, taking belly dancing, reviving her passion for quilting, and getting back into the school system as a consultant. She also traveled to the Middle East, to Doha, Qatar, where she spent a year as an English Content Specialist in an all-girls school.

Ursula asked herself, "What will be my life without teaching?" She toyed with a couple ideas, such as owning a farm and opening a small schoolhouse, but to no avail. Instead, she undertook repairs in her apartment, learned to use a power drill and electric sander, and started managing a small educational grant foundation and working on this book project.

A teacher's life never ends.

BARBARA

Life after Retirement

I was so happy that I had a teaching career. Life can be wonderful and exciting with the promise of carefree time and traveling! However, unexpected things happen which may dramatically alter your perception of what life means.

When my youngest daughter was nineteen, she developed an unusual illness called Guillain-Barre Syndrome, or GBS. She was paralyzed from head to toe and was only able to blink her eyes to communicate. However, even more devastating was the traumatic brain injury that she suffered. In a coma, on a respirator, with her muscles atrophied and suffering cardio respiratory arrest, it left us with little hope of any kind of recovery. However, we never gave up as a family. We kept talking to her, moving her limbs, and playing music to facilitate her recovery.

I thought being a teacher was challenging but little did I know that all my years of teaching would be put to the biggest test of all. After Jane woke up from the coma, my work really began. She was unable to speak, walk, write, do math, and recognize ordinary objects. She did not even know who her father was! My work was clearly marked for me in my retirement. Of course, the doctors said it could be a futile effort but they didn't know Jane and they didn't know us.

When Jane was in a coma, many teachers came to read, talk, and pray for her. Elena, her kindergarten teacher, came several times and comforted me and then spent time talking to Jane and describing the kindergarten class picture that she brought with her and whispering anecdotes about each child into her ear. Several other colleagues visited, talked to her, and helped move her atrophied arms and legs, while also reassuring me that Jane would awake and improve. Some came and prayed with me. The encouragement of my fellow teachers helped me to never give up helping my daughter return to a normal life.

Even though Jane had graduated from high school a few years before, her elementary school teachers would visit her, and some of her high school teachers came to the hospital and read to her from Harry Potter books. Sometimes, the dedication of teachers goes beyond the classroom.

After five weeks, Jane woke up and started to talk. Then my real journey began. She slowly improved, and came home after about seven months. Then, starting from the basic abc's and 123's, and color names, I began my next teaching career, teaching my high school valedictorian and University of Pennsylvania Benjamin Franklin Honors program daughter to learn again!

Jane had intensive physical, occupational, and speech therapy in five different hospitals. But her cognitive therapy was a family responsibility because the doctors didn't think she would benefit from it. However, we stimulated Jane's brain with puzzles, television, movies, and shopping trips to the mall in a wheelchair. Our many, many car trips stimulated her brain and she began to remember places, events, and people. On days that my husband picked me up at school and Jane would be with him, teacher friends would greet Jane at the car with a short anecdote and a sparkle would come into Jane's eyes and she would say, 'Oh, I remember." It was sometimes an exhilarating experience when from nothing a whole scenario would develop in Jane's mind about a particular event in her life before her coma.

So, my retirement has been spent using my teaching skills along with a mother's intuition to re-teach Jane the basic skills all over again. My teaching career came full circle, from teaching hundreds of students to re-teaching my own daughter. Who would have thought thirty-two years ago when I started my career that it would be so instrumental in changing a personal tragedy into a lifelong passion to never give up (because that's what you do when you have a difficult class) and be determined to bring my child back to society and lead an independent and full life. That is what a teacher does!

ELENA

The First Year Out

September 2003. The new school schedule seemed to have been made just for me and my two school-age daughters. For the first time in forever, the school year was beginning with four days of staff development right after Labor Day, and the kids started the following Monday.

What could be better? I did not have to go in to work, the girls had off for four extra days, the rest of the country was already back in school.

Disneyworld!

So, off the three of us flew on a perfect and flawless adventure to *all* the worlds of Disney. No lines at the airport, the rental car seemed to be waiting just for us, complimentary Automobile Club Black Diamond parking upfront, a ride in the driver's cab of the monorail, Mickey waving to us. There was not one line to wait on for four fabulous days of the Magic Kingdom, Epcot, MGM Studios, and the Animal Kingdom. It truly was a magical time and a perfect way to start my retirement.

Then, it was back to the real world. The girls went back to school and I did not have to be anywhere special during the day. Friends who had retired before me told me to be aware of the time warp that occurred upon retiring. And, yes indeed, it was absolutely true.

Here is how it started.

I had cleverly made an 11:00 a.m. dental appointment for the Monday that everyone else went back to school. It probably was the first morning appointment I had ever made in my adult life. I had it prominently displayed on the wall calendar. I had confirmed it on Saturday. When I lingered over my morning coffee, I remembered that it was later in the morning. I went out to do my errands, during the day yet.

And 11:00 a.m. came and went and I was still happily cruising around in the car and missed the appointment. Hours later, it dawned on me. I hurriedly and apologetically called the dental office and was pleasantly told, "Oh don't worry about it, dear, it happens to all the new retirees. See you tomorrow, same time?" I said that I would try to do better.

As the days continued, I discovered the culture of daytime activities in suburbia. I had commuted by car to upper Manhattan for thirty-five years. I left at 6:00 a.m. and got home around 4:00 p.m. Little did I know that during the day, other retirees (mostly older than me) and soccer moms were driving on the local streets slowly, very, very slowly. That was certainly a huge adjustment after decades of the hustle and bustle drive of a commuter.

During the family dinner hour, my partner would ask me, "So, what do you do all day now?" Besides reporting being stuck behind slow drivers, it took me a few months to figure out what I did do all day. Before I retired, in order to do the grocery shopping for the family, my partner and I would go to the supermarket together, usually at the last minute in the evening, divide the chores and be finished in twenty to thirty minutes. It was very hurried yet efficient. We picked familiar brands and stuck to the tried and true family favorites in cereals, protein products, fruits etc.

Then came AR, after retirement. One day, weeks later, when I was asked what I did all day, it dawned on me that the twenty-minute shopping was now taking two hours. I talked to babies in their shopping carts. I helped short elders reach things on high shelves. I discovered that there are seventeen different kinds of aluminum foil. I also had time for my dog, and then for a second one. I was able to attend to my aging mother with delight and patience. I was able to redo the kitchen, paint the house, install laminate flooring, clean the basement and attic, and pull some weeds in the garden. All in all, I pondered, how did I ever have time to work!

Those are the happy memories of the first year out. Then, there are the reflections upon leaving a career that I had loved. I had no regrets. It was just the right time for me. The pension was terrific. The chairs had gotten too small. The new corporate regime began as soon as I left.

On Thursdays, I continued to be a Girl Scout leader in a church right across from the school. I bumped into colleagues and friends. We would chat for a few minutes. They were always glad to see me but not many called me at home or made a date. Out of sight, out of mind. Also, the winds had changed. People were harried and worried.

In school, the rules had instantly changed. Bulletin boards were more important than thinking, product was more important than process. If I had stayed, I probably would have gotten into or made a lot of trouble. Mavericks, rebels, and independent thinkers were deeply frowned upon. I tried going back into the school one or two times but the atmosphere was tight and foreboding. The administration had changed; the security guard was new. I was just another person. So, instead of subjecting myself to any part of this strange environment, I happily busied myself with my family, pets, and meetings with my retired cohorts to begin to write a book.

JACKQUELYNN

Retirement . . . what exactly does that mean? For some, it means packing and moving to a new environment. For others, it means enjoying long-delayed hobbies or pursuits. But, for the large majority, there are no specific plans. For sixteen years, I had participated in a career that gave me much pleasure, challenge, intellectual stimulation, laughter, tears, frustration, and friendship. I sincerely missed the bustling of planning, pulling a new class together, smelling the chalk dust, unwrapping crisp new supplies and books, and the brilliant shine of the school after a long hot summer. (The brilliant shine was thanks to a wonderful, hardworking custodial staff at P.S. 145 that kept our school beaming year round).

There is a physical and emotional adjustment to retirement, especially for teachers. Our year is governed strictly by the calendar. September is the start of a new year with a new lump of clay to sculpt. The holiday breaks offer respite and much-needed rest. And, in June, you send your molded work of art onwards and upwards. Preparing for school in late August, shopping for new materials, books and supplies, eagerly awaiting in the cool, crisp air the new personalities you would spend the better part of a year with, brings a strange comfort or order to the surrounding world.

Once that is over, there is a melancholy that sets in. You no longer have to prepare class lists, sharpen new pencils, sketch out lesson plans, or struggle to create a welcoming bulletin board. Turning off the alarm at 5:30 a.m. and rolling over to sleep without the panic of being late becomes a delicious routine. Gone are the endless administrative meetings, new edicts from the district, now known as regions, and the general routine that is repeated yearly: emergency cards for students, record cards from class to class, transfers, lunch forms, children not yet ready for the return, and anxious parents. All of this ceased to exist for me in my new world.

I actually went cold turkey for the first year, refusing to visit the children's sections of my favorite bookstores. It was as though I was punishing myself. I busied my hours doing exactly what I wanted when I wanted. I took long walks, met for leisure lunches with fellow retiree friends. I began belly dancing classes through the UFT and revived my passion for quilting. This passion, unknown to me at the time, opened another world for me that now results in lectures, as well as teaching quilting to students in NYC schools.

I also began tutoring children of former coworkers and a former student who had left our school several years earlier, just to keep my hand in. Traveling in NYC during nonpeak hours was a delight. I explored museums, finishing long put off household projects (one of which resulted in my good friend Ursula and me laying floors down in my apartment). The first year passed quickly, but life has a way of directing and shaping itself. It might be called destiny, and thus the following began my year out of the box.

In the summer of 2005, my former coworker Carrie had begun working in the Middle East for the Academy of Educational Development. A grant had been awarded to AED to help the Ministry of Education in Qatar to develop an English-speaking curriculum for their schools. She asked if I would submit an application and consider joining her in Doha, Qatar. I did so with her encouragement. On August 30, I returned from my nephew's wedding in Falmouth, Massachusetts, dropped my bags, and caught a very early train to Washington, DC, the next morning for an interview with AED. After a rush of resumes, letters of recommendation, visas, passports, locking up my apartment, and leaving endless instructions for my sister, I found myself, on September 15, sitting on a plane bound for Qatar as their new English Content Specialist. I also realized what I had always known—that I was rich in friends. They had provided recommendations, support, and encouragement quickly and without hesitation.

The Ministry of Education of Qatar had adapted British standards, and schools were systemically phasing in an English curriculum. I was to serve as a consultant to fifteen English-speaking teachers at Safieh Bint Abdulmutallieb Girls' Independent Elementary School. I was thrust into a culture vastly different from any I had visited or grown up in. The education system was even unusual. Teachers taught mostly by rote. I still hear the chanting of lessons by students. My English teachers were women from various areas: Jordan, Egypt, Iraq, Morocco, and Tunisia. The remaining teachers were Qatar natives. The ten-month stay was an adventure. My friend, co-teacher, and coauthor, Ursula, visited for a week, and it was interesting to have her view on this culture. The stay in Qatar exposed me to a culture and religion I had only read about and had been briefly exposed to by my good friends, the Al-Yousefys. I taught two of their children at P.S. 145. Coincidentally, Elena taught them also and we all remain good friends. To live outside of the United States is a broadening experience in many ways. Over the year, I watched teachers affect changes in lesson plans and methods of teaching. Some were very eager to learn anything new. But, like some of our teachers here in the United States, some did the minimum and only went through the motions. I guess people are the same all over. Things I took for granted, like running into Barnes & Noble, Strand, or Bank Street for books were truly missed. In the whole of Doha, there was only one main bookstore, an Office Depot type store that carried a large variety of English books. It was difficult to find English language materials for beginning English. The orders placed for supplies and materials in the summer of 2005 did not arrive until the spring of 2006.

I had the opportunity to visit international schools. These private schools, where expats sent their children, were excellent. After viewing these schools, I wondered why the Qatar government had not taken a look at them as models. In the public schools, there were no teacher education programs at the higher level. They were starting this new curriculum from the bottom up, with teachers who had no formal training in education.

My experiences in Doha are a book in and of itself, which may or may not be shared in written form at a later date. But these experiences and the huge decision to step out of my comfort zone speaks volumes as to the person I had become. For so many years, as a teacher, I had lived in a comfortable cocoon. I had been a risk taker on a very small scale. This was monumental for me. While I had traveled for leisure, I had not really lived abroad. This living not only entailed working, but working in a culture that was dramatically different from the one I grew up in, one that was a religious state and a male-oriented society.

During this first year of my retirement, and a few months beyond, I faced new doors, opened them, and walked through, sometimes more as a learner than teacher.

Once I returned, I took some time to catch up on my year from home. I used the time to reconnect with friends, dancing, quilting, and writing.

In April of 2007, I began working with a university that had developed a professional development department supplying mentors and coaches to low-functioning schools. At this point, I had been out of the public school system for almost three years. This return to the system was a rude awakening. Schools were now in the midst of the NCLB (No Child Left Behind).

As I worked with new teachers, I found they were required to all teach the very same lessons, at the same time. No individuality, no consideration of the needs or personality of the class. It seemed as though the goal for teachers was to quickly work through lessons with the focus of completing a bulletin board at the end of the month. The bulletin board, with its rubric, explanations, and non authentic work had become the holy grail. Teachers seemed to have little opportunity to be creative. Virtually no project work was being done and students were assessed according to the constant testing. Gone was the time for reflection, questioning, discussion, or practice. Students seemed to have very little fun in school or enjoyment in learning. Classrooms were littered with white chart paper of rules and exemplars. Very little student work was evident around in the classroom. There was a growing anger in me as I observed the non education of students that was taking place. Newspapers seem to vilify the profession. The system was being led by businessmen who sent their own children to "good private schools."

I sincerely believe that this ongoing dumbing down of education is purposeful. Parents seem to be not willing to share the responsibility of educating their children, and the UFT has long been guilty of harboring teachers who should have long been expelled from the system.

I now feel like my retirement came at a good time. It does not mean the end of my involvement in education. It is only the opening of new doors.

URSULA

My First Year Out

My retirement happened more suddenly than I had planned. I had always pictured my teaching career to sort of peter out like Ms. Lawson's at Bethesda Community School. She had been in her seventies when I met her and she was still teaching part-time. I was only twenty-three at the time and was to be her eyes and ears, since hers weren't so good any more. But she was wonderful with the children. She confided in me, "I think I would die if I could not teach anymore." What would my life be like without teaching?

Friends and family congratulated me on having "made it." I myself had very mixed feelings about entering this new and inherently last stage of my life, the beginning of the end, as I morosely told myself.

After some initial delays and mix-ups, my retirement checks began to arrive promptly at the beginning of each month. Also, thanks to the persuasion of Lucille, our former union rep at P.S.145, I had begun to contribute to my tax deferred annuity (TDA). This now made all the difference between getting by and enjoying retirement.

So, why was I not ecstatic?

There had been times in my life when I knew exactly what I would do if I were retired. At one time, I thought I wanted to buy a farm. To prepare myself for this, I worked on a dairy farm in upstate New York in the summer of 1996. It was a good thing that I tried it out. Oh, I liked the cows all right and did not mind scraping the manure. But it never had struck me so clearly that farming is a twenty-four-hour, seven-day-a-week job. No traveling, not even to the next larger city. Perhaps, once a year, a visit to the county fair. Never before had I been so happy to be back in the city.

Then, there had been the dream of having my own little schoolhouse. But, teaching the multiage class at P.S. 145 had pretty much fulfilled that wish.

Being anxious about what to do next, I made a deal with myself not to rush into anything but to give myself at least half a year before making any big decisions. In the meantime, little projects started to materialize.

Spending more time at home made me more aware of possible improvements to my apartment. I started by painting the bedrooms and, since then, I have also renovated the kitchen and painted the bathrooms and my very long hallway. I learned how to tile and how to use a wet saw. I am the proud owner of a power drill and an electric sander. I have become a fairly good handywoman. I helped Jackie put down new floors in her apartment and, in the process, learned how to use a power saw, taught by Elena. It seemed we all were involved in home improvement projects. We helped each other and learned from each other.

As a retirement present, I had bought myself a new sewing machine. I made curtains for the newly painted rooms. Afterwards, I made quilts for my grandchildren. I rediscovered the joy of knitting. I started a knitting club at the Young Women's Leadership School in East Harlem.

I also took on the responsibility of setting up and administering a teacher grant for a small foundation. The grant provides materials for teachers to facilitate special classroom projects and learning activities. We receive about fifty applications a year and fund approximately half of them.

And then, of course, there was our book. My good friend Nathalis, also committed to issues of social justice and a professor at Queens College, came up with the idea to get us newly retired teachers together and to capture our wisdom for future generations. I started to organize monthly meetings for us. I invited all the teachers from P.S.145 who had retired within the last two years, and who no longer worked in any capacity for the Department of Education. At first we were seven, and our meetings often seemed more about reminiscing than about getting the project going. Nathalis attended our sessions regularly. Four of us made the final commitment to the project as we started the long process of putting it all down on paper. Elena suggested for each of us to write on each of our topics and thus present our four different voices. This format worked well. We definitely felt that we complemented each other's reflections.

So far, my retirement has been a time to give back. Still, I ask myself every morning, "Was there something else I was supposed to do with my life?" I vigilantly keep searching for it.

Chapter Nine

Conclusion

Teaching is a journey that begins with uncertainty and ends with skepticism. So why get into teaching? This question invites the reader to reflect critically on the meaning of the act of teaching as well as the meaning of learning. Those who do not do so hold a view of education that is limited to the direct delivery of some preplanned curriculum, and the expectation that students will recite back the information conveyed and perform well on tests.

Teaching is much more complicated than that. Bill Ayers (1993) writes, "The work of a teacher—exhausting, complex, idiosyncratic, never twice the same—is, at its heart, an intellectual and ethical enterprise. Teaching is the vocation of vocations, a calling that shepherds a multitude of other callings. It is an activity that is intensely practical and yet transcendent, brutally matter-of-fact, and yet fundamentally a creative act. Teaching begins in challenge and is never far from mystery" (p. 127).

Teaching is one of the loneliest professions. The first year is often a trial by fire. The neophyte teacher soon realizes that despite all the courses taken in teacher education programs nothing prepares him or her for the reality of being in a classroom. A reflective teacher quickly finds that teaching is a practical activity, best learned in the exercise of it and the thoughtful reflection that must accompany it.

Reflective teachers constantly ask themselves what took place during the last class, what approach would have been best in sharing the information with students. There is an ongoing search for the best pedagogy to create a learning environment that is both rigorous and supportive of students. There is also a constant search for community where they can engage in dialogue, where new ways of thinking emerge.

Self-reflection builds confidence. It unleashes a teacher's creativity. Some teachers waste a great deal of time struggling to stay ahead of students because they assume that knowledge is finite and that teaching is a matter of conveying this limited information to the students. A confident teacher plunges into the unknown and learns in partnership with his or her students. Good teachers teach so that they can learn.

Competent teachers must also be attentive to the micropolitics of the school environment. This implies that a good teacher must read the world around him or her, to avoid falling prey to detrimental forces. The harsh reality is that many schools have structures in place that disempower, deskill, pre-specify teacher's thoughts, and constrain their activities. As a result, the teachers partake in a campaign of their own depersonalization when they see themselves as placeholders and low-level bureaucrats, filling out forms and completing procedures.

Teaching is also physical. Jackquelynn says it best, "You are a caretaker." She took her class on trips to the museums, theaters, and restorations. Timmy, a young fellow who spent time in Ursula's class, came running to her on his graduation day to ask her to fix his necktie. He wanted to look good for the graduation ceremony. Barbara spent a couple of years pushing her rolling cart to carry her math materials to various classes till the principal assigned her a room. Elena made language arts and math games from boxes collected on the weekends from hosiery stores.

Last but not least, teaching is emotional. There is a core belief that precedes every act of good teaching. It is the belief in students' abilities and intelligence. This means that the teachers have confidence and faith in, and admiration for them, and appreciate their strengths. This means that the relationship between the teacher and the students is characterized by love and respect. "Pedagogic love keeps students and teachers open-minded, patient and respectful of differences. There is no conflict between teachers' duty to care and their duty to teach because care is at the heart of the teaching relation." (Metcalfe and Game 2006, p. xiii).

Back to our primary question, what brings people to teaching? It is the belief in the promise of public education, a faith in the capability of and intelligence of children, and an enthusiasm for teaching and learning (Nieto 2006). When external forces challenge that faith and belief, teachers get angry.

Our first year was cathartic because the group members addressed the anger they felt when they left the system feeling that they had become the casualty of the No Child Left Behind policy and its absurdities. As the conversations proceeded, the group members moved beyond their feelings and turned the situation into an opportunity. They quickly realized to their great satisfaction that they went into teaching because they wanted to share their lives with children, and they had had that opportunity in abundance.

Chapter Ten

Reflection

During the three years of conversations on education that the former teachers had, several questions emerged. The four women asked themselves who they were, why they became teachers, what forces shaped them, what it was like teaching and working in schools, etc. Their experiences varied but their commitment to the education of children remained constant. "It is about the children," they kept repeating.

However, in a capitalistic economic system, is education truly about children? Myles Horton, educator and founder of the Highlander Center, reminds us that "all education is a form of action based on some kind of social philosophy." (cited by Ayers 1993, p. ix). Then, the fundamental question is, what does it mean to be a teacher in a capitalistic society and more specifically in the No Child Left Behind era?

The NCLB policy emerges from the American tradition of trying to solve social, political, economic, and cultural problems through education (Cremin 1989). This goes back to the earliest colonists who had to rely upon schools and schoolteachers far more than they did in Europe. Perkinson (1977) writes, "Forced to spend their days securing the basic necessities of life, these pioneer parents had little time to care for their children. Moreover, since their New World lacked the agencies of civilization commonplace in the mother country, parents in the New World feared that their children, if untended, might degenerate into savages—not an unlikely fate in this strange, wild, and dangerous land" (p. 3). It is this faith in education that has led Americans to make unwarranted and sometimes unrealistic demands on education.

Like these teachers, we all enter our career full of aspirations and ready to change the world. Elena, Ursula, Jackie, and Barbara were not any different. Ayers (1993) writes, "People are called to teaching because they love children and youth, or because they love being with them, watching them open up and grow and become more able, more competent, more powerful in the world. They may love what happened to themselves when they were with children, the ways in which they become their best selves" (p. 8). Ursula and company embraced teaching and wanted to make a difference in the lives of children. Teaching was about children, opening their minds, and exposing them to new experiences. In this process, they had to struggle against institutions, procedure-centered places characterized by hierarchy, control, and the cult of efficiency. They realized that the profession is full of people who do not respect its purpose. The frustrations of working with incompetent school administrators was in dark contrast with the joys of seeing children excited about learning.

Here is what Elena wrote: It's about the kids.

HYPOTHETICAL #1

So, what if the first day of school came around and the kids didn't come to school? What would teachers do with all the standards and testing materials and bulletin board guidelines? What would the principals, assistant principals, district honchos, and other hoards of upper echelon, big-salaried personnel do? What about the lunchroom workers, the custodial staff, the family workers, the attendance monitors, guidance counselors, social workers, psychologists, educational therapists, speech pathologists, physical therapists, or occupational therapists? What would they do?

Education has become a corporation, a conglomerate with an immense after-product market. The after-products being the above-mentioned positions. It is about money, money, money, money, make-work positions, and a lot of power brokering.

The building blocks of this conglomerate, namely, the students, have gotten lost in the game.

HYPOTHETICAL #2

So, what if on the first day of school all the kids came but none of the teachers showed up? What would they do with all the standards and testing materials and bulletin board guidelines? Would the principals, assistant principals, district honchos, and other hoards of upper echelon, big-salaried personnel know what to do with one million children for over six hours a day? Would bulletin boards and testing materials be so important then? Now, management becomes the biggest issue. Educational theory and practice would be on hold. They would not be able to handle it successfully.

HYPOTHETICAL #3

So, what if on the first day of school the kids and the teachers come to school and all the others are absent. Eureka, it would work! The experts on education and management would be there and the kids who are the object of education would have their mentors. But wait, there used to be a model similar to this. Oh yes, it was the one-room schoolhouse, one teacher and a bunch of kids. In our system of corporate education, the children have gotten lost. There are so many pressures and rules and regulations and demands applied arbitrarily and mostly without pedagogic relevance that the amount of time the children have with their teachers is minimal.

Six-plus hours minus fifty minutes for lunch, fifty minutes for prep, and tens of accumulated minutes taken away by loudspeaker announcements, interruptions by officials with clipboards assessing progress, children being pushed in or pulled out, fire drills, emergency drills, irate parents, irate administrators, disruptive children, moving to and from activities, and bathroom expeditions equals a day of instructional time of probably four hours. In those four hours, four periods are mandated for literacy and math. So, when do the other four subject areas, science, social studies, art, music (not to mention a truly meaningful Phys. Ed. Program) fit in? They don't. Reading and math are all that count. Why? They can be standardized and tested and then administrators can receive fatter bonus checks and the classrooms will still not have pencils, except on test day.

The kids are being shortchanged by corporate education. They are receiving superficial and shallow instruction.

So, what to do? Close your classroom door. Dig deep. Go back to basics. Compact and integrate the curriculum. Teach all the curriculum areas. Figure out what paperwork is essential. Put the rest on the pile until it is called for the third time. Smile and nod and say, "Oops, I forgot." Pretend you are in your own little red schoolhouse and it is just you and the kids. Take a chance, take a stand, do the right thing.

Jackie wrote: It is about the children.

Teachers, administrators, and parents often forget, it's about the children. They forget that they, themselves, not too long ago, were children. They forget their own school years. However, in that fog of forgetfulness, if asked the name of their favorite teacher it will quickly roll off their tongue. I would like to think that down the road I became someone's favorite teacher. Each year, and sometimes mid-year, a child will enter your classroom with wonder, exhilaration, and excitement. It is each child's first, unique experience in that grade. It is up to the teacher to provide that wonderment.

I so very well remember my favorite teacher. I was fortunate to have her in fourth and sixth grades of elementary school. Mrs. Englander, a World War II war bride. I never knew what that meant! She was tall, thin, with shoulder-length brown hair that unfortunately did not cover her ears. She was impeccably groomed with two-piece tailored suits, always a lovely piece of jewelry, hanky, gloves, and a fox wrap draped around her shoulders. This fur piece intrigued the entire class because it was the head of a fox that bit its tail to encircle Mrs. Englander. While she was strict, she was extremely kind and sensitive. She had the ability to make every child in her class feel special. Above all, she was fair to all of us.

From the mid-1940s through 1952, I attended a progressive elementary public school (P.S. 99), filled with a mixture of all kinds of children of diverse ethnic backgrounds: Whites, Blacks, Jews, Puerto Ricans, Irish, Italians. This chorus of nine-year-olds followed Florence Englander into the world of wonderment. It seemed as if we wandered from theme to theme and had to literally be torn away. She had the ability to make the day flow effortlessly. I learned about the settlement of New York by the Dutch by illustrating glass slides for an audiovisual presentation, and studied about Native Americans by recreating villages and making papier mâché masks. I do not know if she ever knew the effect she had on her students and their future. I remember that she took the time out to learn about her students in her classroom. She was extremely nurturing. I remember being made to suffer through making a Father's Day card every year except in her class. She realized my father had passed away and kindly suggested I make a card for my grandfather or uncle instead.

I have only met one other student, who like me, was in her fourth-grade class, who remembered her. That student moved away in mid-term but Mrs. Englander continued to write and encourage him. It is not surprising he went on to become a successful African-American attorney.

So, I return to the phrase, it's about the children. I wish every child could be taught by a Mrs. Englander. I think in many ways I based much of my teaching skills on the memories of her class. I had two years of that wonderfulness. It would be great if each child were able to take away two things from each class they attended: something wonderful they have learned and the best day they have had in the class. Teachers need to remember it is the child's first experience in that grade.

I look back over my school days and the classrooms of today. There is such a notable absence of art, music, crafts, and so on, today. Mrs. Englander was able to incorporate all of the above. I do not know if she was hampered by the administration. I do feel we moved at a much slower pace. We were able to eat, chew, and digest, rather than open and swallow the curriculum as offered. I am sure we had the standardized tests; however, they were not the primary focus as they are today.

I have often wondered why there was not a children's forum on what it was that children liked about school. I have often observed and taken a cue from my students about the things they were interested in. Several years prior to my retiring, there was a mandate to use only "prescribed materials" for reading and math. All other sets of readers and math books were to be "thrown away." I figuratively had a heart attack at just the thought of throwing books in the garbage. What a waste! Throughout the years, I had used a set of anthologies that worked. They were challenging as well as child-friendly. These colorful books contained a variety of reading genres, but the most important fact was that the students loved these books. I often would find a child reading ahead and nagging me, "When are we going to read the next story?" Without any prompting, they would find examples, make comparisons, and write different endings, and so on. I resorted to stealth methods to carefully store them away during vacations because, indeed, the new regime had thrown away tons of books. I would instruct my students to keep them inside their desks, out of sight, when not in use. This worked in the math area also. When moving to a new math program, I found the older books simpler for some students. I remember vividly that one of my students completed a whole math workbook mistakenly as a homework assignment.

So much of teaching is fraught with fighting against the nature of children. Perhaps it would be more constructive to go along with the children and their developmental growth, their desire for and interest in learning.

Elena, Ursula, Barbara, and Jackie vested over a century in the New York public school system. They all retired in the first years of the new millennium. Their retirement coincided with the signing into law of the No Child Left Behind Act (NCLB) on January 8, 2002, by President Bush. This act contained the most sweeping changes to the Elementary and Secondary Education Act (ESEA) enacted in 1965.

The NCLB Act provides money for extra educational assistance to children who need it, in return for improvement in their academic progress. States willing to receive federal NCLB funds must agree to the law's requirements to establish learning standards and provide a statement of what children in that particular state should know and be able to do in reading, math, and other subjects, at various grade levels. The state must develop annual assessments to measure students' progress in reading and math in grades three through eight. The state must set a level of proficiency in the tested areas and make public the results of that testing in terms of what percentage of students meet the requirement. This information is sorted by race, income, disability, language proficiency, and gender (Meister 2007).

There are four basic education reform principles as stated in the NCLB: (1) stronger accountability for results, (2) increased flexibility and local control, (3) expanded options for parents, and (4) an emphasis on teaching methods proven to work. The goal of the NCLB is that all students will become proficient in reading and math by 2014. Proponents of this law make the case that, for the first time, teachers are being asked to show that their students are learning. This request has been trumpeted as something that has never been done before. Some skeptics have said that the emphasis on raising the achievement in all groups was a noble goal, but it was being executed ineptly. They argued that one could not make something happen just by declaring that it must (Meister 2007).

Opponents of the NCLB have argued that this law handcuffs educators and disarms them of their creativity. It forces them to teach to the test. They also observe that the law punishes teachers and administrators who try to help the neediest kids. It narrows the curriculum. It begs schools and districts to lower standards and set unrealistic expectations. It looks like education policy makers have not learned anything from history. The school system is being sent back to a corporate model of management, where the priority on economic efficiency is nothing less than the "factoryization" of education, under which the teacher becomes "an automaton, a mere factory hand, whose duty it is to carry out mechanically and unquestioningly the idea and orders of those with authority of position and who may or may not know the needs of children or how to minister to them." (Haley 1904, p. 312).

Maxine Greene (1973), teacher-philosopher, writes, "The teacher who wishes to be more than a functionary cannot escape the value problem or the difficult matter of moral choice" (p. 181). Teachers are routinely made into functionaries. Schools tend to disempower and deskill teachers by pre-specifying teachers' thoughts, overseeing them, and constraining their activities. Teachers become docile by conforming, following the rules, and delivering curriculum without much thought or control of the students. The lessons learned from such an environment is about hierarchy and one's place in it, convention and one's obligation to it, and unquestioning passivity in the face of authority (Ayers 1993).

The NCLB was well intended but poorly thought out and implemented. Focusing on high-stakes testing is neither something that teachers are used to nor willing to comply with. In many schools, it has turned administrators into enforcers rather than educators. Veteran teachers are being told how to teach. Slowly, but surely, education has become no longer about children but about passing the test. It is against this background that Elena, Ursula, Jackie, and Barbara retired. They felt that the new educational policy impacted on their love for teaching and made teaching impossible for them, especially when their commitment was first and foremost to the children rather than to the state.

This is not the first time the US educational system has been on cruise-control reform. Beginning in the eighties, with the publication of *A Nation at Risk,* the leadership of this country felt that more needed to be done in the school system to face up to the international competition led by Japan and Germany. *A Nation at Risk* was the beginning of the excellence movement in the school system. From this movement, we moved to the standards movement and recently to the choice movement, always in search of something that no one could really define.

However, what emerges from the teachers' narratives is that the NCLB law is not about the education of children, it is about training a highly skilled workforce that will help the United States compete in the global economy. To prepare such a workforce, the economy needs docile minds and docile bodies who will dedicate themselves entirely to the capitalistic economic system. In this scheme, there is no need for critical thinking skills, self-reflection, and questioning. Obedience is greatly appreciated.

Teachers on their part focus on the intellectual, behavioral, and moral development of children. They want them to have fun, play, learn, and enjoy. For the teachers, education is first and foremost about the cognitive and affective development of children. They believe that developing these skills makes one useful to society because these skills are essential in the workforce.

Thus, there exists a tension between policy makers and teachers, concerning their beliefs about education. While teachers insist that it is about the children, the powers that be insist that it is about competing in the new economy. How do we reconcile this tension and find a middle ground so that not everything is about global competition but some things are about personal development without neglecting our socioeconomic and political system?

The paradox of educational reform in the United States is that it is always initiated from the top down. Teachers who know their schools and their students including the neighborhoods in which they work are never invited to the table. They constantly find themselves in situations where they have to meet mandates that, in many instances, do not benefit their students nor themselves but instead protect the school administrators who can no longer be educators but become enforcers of the law.

Let's consider these arguments one at a time. In his classic *The Sorting Machine,* Joel Spring argues that, since 1945, the federal government of the United States has played an increasing role in the conduct of educational institutions. The cold war and the demands of the civil rights movement pushed the federal government to order the schools to focus on training people for meeting the manpower needs of the cold war and the economic development of the country. Proponents of this policy argued that public education could increase the efficiency of industrial society by proper selection and channeling of national manpower.

This was the return to the cult of efficiency. This whole argument supported the rise of vocational guidance, the grouping of students according to ability, the separation of students in high school into different academic programs according to future occupations, and the importance of intelligence testing. This argument allowed schools to determine students' abilities and channel them through programs that the school judges decided would best fit their career aspirations. The schools became sorting machines. It is this argument that justified the involvement of the federal government in education, a direct concern about meeting the manpower needs in the cold war and the demands of the civil rights movement.

Today, the same argument is being replayed, not in the name of the civil rights movement but rather in the name of globalization. The need for a high-skills workforce has never been as crucial. Because of the lack of a highly skilled workforce, companies in the United States are outsourcing their jobs overseas, where labor is highly skilled and cheaper. We have a situation where, to give just one example, computer programmers and technicians overseas read X-rays of patients in the United States.

Slowly but surely, our workforce is being deskilled and our jobs are disappearing. It is indeed a crisis and a mess. But it is also an opportunity that begs for imagination, creativity, and bold solutions.

We all have something to say about education. This is a problem. Competent teachers know children want instructors who know their subject matter, motivate and excite them, make learning fun. Children want teachers who know them and their parents. Most importantly, they want teachers who understand how they learn and adjust their teaching style to their learning style. Children are capable of high and sophisticated levels of thinking and writing. To unleash this capacity, their imagination and intelligence must be engaged. Respect for teachers, students, parents is at the core of good education.

Students We Remember

BARBARA

The best thing about being a teacher is working with children. It is not about impressing people with the career that you have chosen. In my thirty-four years of teaching, I had the privilege of working with young minds. I hoped to teach them their academic skills as well as to be lifelong learners.

Even though I taught hundreds of students, some became a permanent part of my memory.

How can I forget Vivian? She was in my fourth-grade class in the late 1960s. Vivian lived with her grandmother. She was responsible for taking care of her younger brother. She had a vivid imagination. This is a nice way of saying she lied all the time. Her grandmother had to be called so we could separate fact from fiction. Vivian was always in trouble, rarely did her work, and constantly required attention. After a tumultuous year in my class, she managed to graduate. The biggest surprise was when Vivian came back to see me seven years later. I will never forget what she said, "I am sixteen. I never took drugs. I was never pregnant. I stayed in school and I stayed out of trouble." Vivian made my day! I felt that in some small way my concern about her helped her develop into a responsible teenager.

Then there was Richard. He was in another of my fourth-grade classes. Richard was quiet and unassuming. He tried hard but never became an outstanding student. Many years later, after I was married and the mother of three, I went to a New Jersey mall to buy sneakers for my children. We went to a Footlocker and I was very tired so I sat on a bench immediately outside the store. Suddenly, a very good-looking young man came out, screaming at the top of his lungs, pointing at me, saying, "She was my fourth-grade teacher!" He told me he never forgot me and that he was the manager of the

131

store and was married with two children. What a wonderful surprise for me. I learned that you never know which student you will have the greatest effect upon!

Another wonderful experience happened on 34th Street in front of the Empire State Building. I was waiting for a bus when a well-dressed young man came up to me and told me that I had been his fourth-grade teacher. He was married and worked in the Empire State Building. Again, I was rewarded by the fact that he remembered me.

Then there was Rudy. He was a very difficult child. He was in my class when I was pregnant with my second child. He literally tested my patience. He was very disruptive and not motivated to do schoolwork. However, he had a very cooperative and understanding mother who worked with me, and together we were able to put Rudy on the right track, and his behavior and work began to improve. Many years later, after I had retired, I met Rudy in Manhattan. He was having difficulty seeing the time readout on a parking meter because it was dark. My husband happened to lend him a flashlight that he carried to read parking meters in the dark. All of a sudden, Rudy noticed me as I approached our car, and we were overcome with emotion. He was married to a lovely lady and was visiting his father in the hospital nearby. He remembered me after all of those years. The unexpected meeting was both a rewarding and touching moment for me!

These students are just a sample of the hidden treasures that come with teaching. The influence that teachers have on students can never be measured in terms of money or prestige. It is the personal, human-to-human relationship that is truly special and more rewarding than one can ever imagine. When Richard came running out of Footlocker with his finger pointing at me, screaming that I was his fourth-grade teacher, I finally felt like a rock star.

ELENA

I taught for thirty-five years. Eighteen were in kindergarten, ten in second grade, one in fourth grade, four in first grade, and two as Lillian Weber's first ever Open Corridor teacher. Multiply all those years by twenty-five students as an average (from forty-two first graders in the financially strapped 1970s to the year when I had fourteen kindergartners) and it appears that I have taught almost one thousand kids in my classes.

That seems like a little for all those years but it also seems like a lot. Do I remember them all, sadly, no. Do they all remember me, probably not. But do I remember some, yes. I remember many. Why do some remain in the recesses of my mind? It is a mystery. Some were terrific kids, some really funny, some really sad, some really troubled.

So, as a reflection on my long life as a classroom teacher, I end our journey with remembrances of some of those I can remember and with apologies to those I cannot.

Bobby, 1970. He came to school every day with his big smile and great eagerness to learn and with his hungry belly and his very dirty clothes. We spent many a lunch time at the laundromat. He would sit wrapped in a blanket and I had lots of quarters. He had to go home in his own clothes because his mother did not take charity.

Lori, 1980. She was smarter than smart and a survivor. Her mother died of AIDS, I am sure. She died of AIDS even before the general population knew what AIDS looked like, because in retrospect and with the images we now recognize, that's how Lori's mother looked. Thomas, 1976. I don't remember Thomas at all as having been one of my students. But he remembered me. In 1995, I was taking my wiggly group of kindergartners to the lunchroom one day and I was very distracted. I felt a gentle tap on my shoulder and a tall, handsome, well-dressed young man said, "Hi, you were my second-grade teacher. My name is Thomas. I am a substitute teacher here today." We chitchatted for a few moments. I called him "honey," wished him good luck, offered any help I could give, we hugged and said, "See you later," and I never saw him again.

May, 1996. She was a bright and articulate girl, happy and curious, with a great sense of humor. During every year in kindergarten, we worked on using "May I" appropriately and tried to do away with the awkward backwards phrasing of "I can play?" Every time a child would ask me in the "I can?" format, I would say "May I" back to them. Over the months, my response became an exasperated "May," and she would answer from the other side of the room, "Yes, Elena, did you want me?" The two of us would laugh, we got it.

Sandra, 1975. At the end of June 2003, after school was over for the year, with every paper and document I ever could possibly need in a bulging briefcase (so that there would be no mistakes), I went to the infamous Worth Street office to file my retirement papers, barely breathing for the hour that the bureaucratic process took.

I walked out of the Teachers' Retirement Office and danced joyfully while waiting for the slow elevator. I must have been beaming as I entered the elevator already occupied by a chubby, friendly-looking, fortyish woman. She probably thought I was nuts. She looked at me and seemed familiar with the ebullient look of new retirees because she worked in the building, and said, "Oh my God, you're Ms. Dubovick" (my original last name). I looked at her and immediately said, "You're Sandra." We hugged and kissed each other. Laughing, remembering, and filling in the blanks of the past thirty years. We walked out onto the boiling hot June sidewalk. Before we parted, she asked me what I remembered about her when she was in my second-grade class all those many years before. It took less than a nanosecond for my response, "Sandra, you had the skinniest legs!" and she answered, "Yes, I did."

URSULA

This is a poem by one of my third grade students. He wrote it a few days after he had been moved into my class from another third grade.

> "The Classroom"
> I'm happy about my class
> I love my class
> They're helpful
> They're full of joy
> They are full of joy
> They are!

As expressed in this poem, learning should be a joyous experience. Schools and classrooms should be kind, thoughtful, intellectually stimulating, physically and emotionally safe places. But, for many children, sadly, it is not. Children need to feel loved and appreciated in order to feel safe. And children need to feel safe in order to freely and successfully engage in learning.

More than a thousand children have been in my care during the many years of my teaching and each child has a story. Their stories will always be part of my life. Many of my students have disappeared into their own lives but my memories of them always remain. Surprisingly, though, some still cross my path and sometimes in unexpected places.

There is Vincent who works at the 99 Cents store in our school neighborhood. When he told his boss that I was his teacher, his boss would not believe him. Vincent and I look more like former classmates than teacher and student. I think his life has not been easy. He is a very hard worker and he is always extra nice to me. "Teacher, what can I do for you today?"

One of my students is a principal and a few are teachers. I know of one who became a social worker. Another is a filmmaker. One student has a PhD in multimedia applications. He gave me a copy of his dissertation and, needless to say, I can't understand a word of it. A dollar bill was stuck inside. When he was around ten years old, I bet him a dollar that he would get a PhD. His dedication reads, "For Ursula who knew about this dissertation long before I did."

Two of my students have died. One was shot about a block away from the school in a drug deal gone foul. Another one died of AIDS that he contracted as an intravenous drug user. One of my students is in prison on murder charges.

Then there is Leo, my second-grade student who, nine years ago, asked me to hold his journals. "I'll get them later," he said. And now, even though I am retired, I'm still holding these journals for Leo. Every so often I look at them. His handwriting was neat and his spelling and grammar up to par. He liked to draw and was pretty good at it. Most of his journal entries start with "Today I'm going to," with typical variations of either "my mom's house," "my grandma's house," "my aunt's house," or sometimes, "today after school I'll visit my dad." Leo stayed in many places. After his opening sentence, "Today I'm going to . . ." he usually wrote about what he was going to do at a particular place, who was going to be there, and who would play with him. He often wrote as much as a whole page. Tucked into one of his journals is a picture of his great-grandmother taken by Leo as part of a homework assignment for one of our photography projects. She was a very important presence in his life.

By the end of second grade, Leo's father was back in jail and, a few years later, his great-grandmother died. Every so often I bump into Leo in the neighborhood. By now, he is much taller than I am. He always greets me with a smile and we hug each other. The young men that are usually with him look puzzled and slightly embarrassed at this hugging scene in the middle of Amsterdam Avenue. He introduces me, "Yeah, she is my old teacher. I had her in second grade." He was implying that I was OK. I often wonder where Leo stays these days. When I ask him how it's going, he tells me, "I'm fine, I'm fine." Before we part, I always remind Leo, "I still have your journals. You let me know when you want them." And he always tells me, "You hold on to them for me." I hope that one day he'll tell me, "I'll come and get them."

For Leo, our classroom was more than a school room. It was his second home. We were his school family and he needed a teacher who taught him more than the basics. He needed one who showed him how to be a mensch. So far so good, Leo has been able to stay in school all these years.

While I was rummaging through Leo's old journals, I came across a home-made card from another student, Trish. It was made from purple construction paper, with a bright pink Valentine pasted on the outside and a yellow sun drawn in the right-hand corner. It looked like something Trish might have made during free time. "I Love You" was written on the cover and on the inside it said, "I love you mom." On the back of the card, I had made a note, "1/21/98. Trish gave me this card today. She said I know it says mom, but you are like my mom too." I do not remember what prompted this card. Perhaps everybody was making cards for their moms and Trish wanted to do what everybody else was doing. Also, young children sometimes accidentally call their teacher "mom," but usually do not make that mistake in writing. Trish was in foster care at the time and I might have been the best person to give the card to. Trish desperately wanted to have somebody she could call her own mom. I remember a visit from her case worker during class. Trish would have loved for her caseworker to be her mom. She did not move from her caseworker's side the whole time she was visiting. Later, she explained to the class that she has a caseworker "just in case." I hoped that she would never discover that having a caseworker makes you a case. All she wanted to be was a little girl who was loved.

When I first started teaching, I had a little girl, Uschi, in my kindergarten in Germany. On the first day of school, her mother approached me and said apologetically, "Uschi sucks her thumb all day. We have tried everything but to no avail." I told her not to worry, that she would probably forget about it in school. Well, Uschi did not. I still can see her sitting in one of our little chairs, totally absorbed in sucking her thumb. She did not play, she did not talk. She was too preoccupied with her thumb. My son was a six-month-old baby at the time and I always carried a supply of pacifiers around with me. Having watched Uschi suck her thumb for weeks and not be able to engage with the materials or talk with the other children, I impulsively grabbed a pacifier, still in its store wrapper. I offered it to her. She took it, smiled at me, and put the pacifier in her mouth. Now, she had her hands free to play and she was very happy. As she got more and more engaged with the materials, and eventually with the other children, she used the pacifier less and less. Some weeks later, Uschi's mother showed up at the classroom door gesturing toward me and saying, "I want to talk to you." The pacifier arrangement had been between Uschi and me. Somehow, we had managed for the other forty-five children not to pay much attention to it.

And now, here was Uschi's mother. "You've been caught, Ursula," went through my mind, and I quickly tried to think of ways to defend myself. I was not prepared for what happened next. Uschi's mother took a beautiful, brand new picture book out of her bag. "This is a present for you and the class. Uschi has been like a different child these last few weeks. I don't know how you did it. We are so thankful." I never told the mother about the pacifier, why rock the boat? Would I do this today? Definitely not! I would get into big trouble!

Recently, I ran into another old student in a neighborhood shoe store. We recognized each other and Robin introduced me to her coworkers, "This is Ms. Foster, my fourth-grade teacher." And then, hesitantly, she added, "I gave her a hard time." And indeed she had. But not as hard a time as she had given her father and his girlfriend. "I have changed," she added. "I'm not like that anymore." Robin had a baby when she was quite young and that changed her. She really wanted to be a good mom. Her little baby boy somehow helped her to become a better person.

Since I am now retired I enjoy frequent visits to the Metropolitan Museum of Art and I do some of my gift shopping in their children's gift shop. Luckily for me, another student of mine, Keith, works there and always offers me his 25 percent discount. If things are not too busy at the gift shop, he gives me an update on his music career. It is very nice to have a friend at my favorite museum.

And then there was Leila. I will always remember Leila. Before she entered my first grade, her kindergarten teacher came to me to tell me about this very special little girl. She explained, "I recommended her for the Gifted and Talented Program but her mother did not take her for the test. She is so bright and she needs so much support."

Leila did well in first grade. She learned to read, she enjoyed drawing, and writing stories. She was well liked by her classmates.

Two years later, I moved to teach second grade. To my great surprise, I found Leila as a holdover on my second-grade class list. Leila, smart Leila, a holdover?

In September, at the first opportunity, I took Leila aside and asked her, "What happened to you in second grade?" I had previously asked her former second-grade teacher the same question. The teacher had dismissively grumbled, "Leila didn't do any work all year long, she was late every single day, and she never listened." Didn't he know that little Leila was the one who got herself ready for school? Of course, sometimes her socks didn't match but what do you expect from a seven-year-old? Didn't he know that Leila often came to school without breakfast? The school's breakfast program is fine for children who get to school on time but not for the ones that are twenty minutes late. Didn't he know that Leila had to be independent and strong-minded in order to survive?

Leila's answer to my question matched her teacher's: "I didn't do any work." "Why Leila," I asked. And she answered, "Because he didn't like me."

At the end of the school year, when Leila was ready to move on to third grade, I pleaded with her, "Please Leila, please do your work next year, even if the teacher doesn't like you." Leila thought for a while and then answered, "I have to be honest, Ursula, I can't promise." Leila got lucky though. Her third-grade teacher appreciated her too.

Leila's story made me reminiscent of my college application essay in which I wrote, "In order for a teacher to be effective, she has to regard her students as her very personal future." Leila brought back the long ago memory of my mission statement of commitment and hope.

During her remaining years at P.S.145, Leila visited my class on days when her teacher was absent. On one of those occasions, Leila joined us in a poetry-writing workshop. She wrote (and sadly, I only remember the beginning of her poem):

Let me be
Let me be me
Let me be the way I am

While trying to find the "Let me be" poem, another of Leila's poems surfaced.

If I were a kite
I could fly in the sky so high
And go to adventures
You would not even know.
I will turn back around
And say good bye

When we are with our students, their hearts and souls and minds are entrusted to us. We must nurture them with the utmost care. Schools play a very important role in the socialization of children. Children need to experience themselves as important and contributing members of their classroom community. Yet, sometimes, teachers are often callous when assigning children their roles.

I hope I taught my students well about kindness and caring, about being responsible and dependable. I might end up in one of the three Homes for the Aged in my neighborhood where one of my students might be my caregiver.

Each and every child is our very personal future. To raise and educate them well should be our first priority.

JACKQUELYNN

I boarded the bus recently and as I settled into my seat, a woman with a vaguely familiar face plopped down beside me and said, "Ms. Jones! You planted a good seed!" I was slightly taken aback as she went rushing on about her daughter, Melissa. Melissa was in my second- and third-grade G&T class. Her mom went on to say she consistently held high grade averages, was on the honor roll, and was a hard worker. She said, "Those two years Melissa spent with you set her on the right track, helped her to develop good study habits that she has carried with her." I explained to her that we were a team. I remember Melissa's mom went the extra mile to encourage her.

Unlike Elena, Ursula, and Barbara who have taught twice as long as I have, my students are just about coming into adulthood. In my mind, they remain frozen in time . . . still first, second, and third graders. If they remained at our elementary school, I silently watched them grow for two or three more years. I have often wondered about their futures, their personal well-being, and their families. Frequently, the relationship was extended when a sibling or cousin found themselves in my class.

Throughout the years I have run into some of my past students. Some families have become friends and I have had the privilege of watching these children as they have made their way from elementary, through middle school, and into their first years of college.

There has been Caroline, who is in her first year of high school, and Kia, who headed to Tufts University, and, of course, Michael. I mention these three children because as the diversity of our West Side community changed, these children, who are white, had extremely strong families that did not bow to public opinion, neighborhood pressure, or stereotyping gossip. They chose to keep their children in their neighborhood school. When I look back on it, these children often walked in the same shoes I so often do, that is, being the solitary minority in a particular situation. When I questioned Caroline's mother one day about the situation, her reply to me was that Caroline needed to learn to work and understand all kinds of people, regardless of their ethnicity, economic level, etc. That is the future world she will live in. As I write this last chapter, Barack Obama, our first African American president is giving his first Presidential Address to Congress. It is truly the world that Caroline, Michael, and Kia and all our children will inherit.

While my students have remained frozen in my mind, they have gone on with their lives. They occasionally write and tell me they are moving on to the next level. They often tell me news of other students in their class. Joseph, a cheerful, happy young man, full of mischief, recently appeared in the movie Doubt with Meryl Streep. I'd known that he had been in the theatre and appeared in a few films. I am pleased that he is now pursuing this gift seriously. There is Aja, who stunned me years ago, sitting on the floor at age four reading a chapter book while her mom was working with the Girl Scouts. She finally arrived in my third-grade class with her whispery voice that hid the talents of a nightingale. Last June, I attended Aja's high school graduation as she headed off to college. I also correspond with Serena who is considering going to boarding school. She says she thinks it will help her grow and become more independent.

As I visited the movies one afternoon, a striking young woman asked if I was Ms. Jones. When I said yes and asked her name, she said excitedly, "Tiffany! I was in Ms. Foster's class! Do you remember when we made the gingerbread houses for Christmas?" I paused for a moment, my mind like a computer, trying to place her. I vaguely remembered her being tall, thin, with braids. It is hard seeing her now fully grown. She was working as a theatre manager part-time as she attended college. I am glad her memories of me were happy ones that she has carried all these years.

I often visit Maha and Mohammed A., whose parents are from Yemen. These two children and their families help make up the tapestry of America. I have admired that they have been gracious enough to share their culture and traditions with me.

Mrs. A. had always been one of those parents who provided parental support in the classroom. When I spent a year in the Middle East, she provided much personal and emotional support and encouragement. When I needed samples of my student's work, Mohammed's portfolio traveled from New York to Doha, Qatar, as an example of exemplary classroom work.

I often think of the children who encountered personal tragedies and wonder what became of them. There was J., whose father passed away of AIDS in my first grade; L, who could charm you with his smile, but was so troubled, and C., who was so full of anger. I often hear that many have persevered. Others have not.

Years ago, in a supermarket, I ran into a familiar young woman. She was ringing up my groceries. She kept her head down, seemingly not wanting to make eye contact. A little girl came up to her, pulling on her skirt."Mommy, Mommy." She quietly hushed her. I looked at her name tag and realized she had been in one of my classes when I taught at the School for Writing and Publishing. I remember she was a brilliant writer, but so full of anger and self-destruction. I also knew her home life was difficult and she received little encouragement. As I looked at her daughter, I realized she was far too young to be a mother. My student was living a life of the "dream unfulfilled." We chatted a bit and she remembered me. She smiled and we parted. I often wonder about that encounter. How many other students are living a dream unfulfilled? I sincerely hope that most of my students have had their dreams fulfilled.

At my retirement party, one of the students from my very first class came to say good-bye. I remember K. well. He was painfully thin, with his Catholic school belt pulled too tight to hold up his pants. I think he sensed I was new to the game. He pulled every trick in the book! He was a good escape artist during the reading period. But I soon became adept to his tricks. K. came over to say thank-you. He had become an entrepreneur and had started three businesses. When he was in the fourth grade, I received a letter from him. He wrote to tell me he was leaving the fourth grade and "if you had not stuck with me, I would not be going to fifth grade."

Hopefully, I planted "good seeds."

References

Ayers, William. 1993. *To teach: The journey of a teacher.* New York: Teachers College Press.

Berliner, David C. 1986. In pursuit of the expert pedagogue. *Educational Researcher* 15,7:5–13.

Blasé, Jo J. 1987. Political interactions among teachers: Socio-cultural context in the schools. *Urban Education* 22:286–309.

———. 1985. The socialization of teachers: An ethnographic study of factors contributing to the rationalization of the teacher's instructional perspective. *Urban Education* 20:235–256.

Bourdieu, Pierre. 1977. *Outline of a theory of practice.* Cambridge, MA: Cambridge University Press.

Bowles, Samuel, and Herbert Gintis. 1976. *Schooling in capitalistic America.* New York: Basic Books.

Boyer, Ernest L. March 27, 1993. Making the connection. Speech delivered at the Annual Conference of the Association for Supervision and Curriculum Development, Washington, DC.

Coleman, James S. 1966. *Equality of educational opportunity.* Washington, DC: US Government Printing Office.

Collins, Marva. Biography, http://www.marvacollins.com (accessed December 2, 2008)

Covey, Stephen. 1990. *Principle-centered leadership.* New York: Simon & Schuster.

Cremin, Lawrence A. 1989. *Popular education and its discontents.* New York: Harper and Row Publishers.

Delpit, Lisa. 1995. *Other people's children. Cultural conflict in the classroom.* New York, NY: The New Press.

Dewey, John. 1929. *The quest for certainty: A study of the relation of knowledge and action.* New York: Minton, Balch.

———. 1916. *Democracy and education..* New York: The Free Press.

Einhardt, G., R.T. Putnam, M.K. Stein, and J. Baxter. 1991. Where subject knowledge Matters. In *Advances in research on teaching,* ed. J. Brophy, 2:87–113. Greenwich, CT: JAI.

Escalante, Jaime. Biography, http://boliviaweb.com/hallfame/escalante.htm. (accessed December 2, 2008).

Freire, Paulo. February 4, 1993. Teaching and learning. Paper presented at the California Association for Bilingual Education, Anaheim, CA.

Gibson, Linda. 1998. Teaching as an encounter with the self: Unraveling the mix of personal beliefs, education ideologies, and pedagogical practices. A*nthropology and Education Quarterly* 29,3:360–371.

Greene, Maxine. 1973. *Teacher as a stranger.* Belmont, CA: Wadsworth.

Griffin, Gary A., ed. 1999. *The education of teachers: Ninety-eighth yearbook of the National Society for the Study of Education.* Chicago: University of Chicago Press.

Gordon, Donalson. 2001. *Cultivating leadership in schools: Connecting people, purpose and practice.* New York: Teachers College Press.

Haley, Margaret. 1904. Why teachers should organize. *Addresses and proceedings of the National Education Association,*148–151.

Heath, Shirley. B. 1983. *Ways with words: Language, life and work in communities and classrooms.* Cambridge, UK: Cambridge University Press.

Heinstra, Roel J. 2006. Competent teachers. Trans. Joop Gankema and Doug Springate, http://www.lerarenweb.nl. (accessed June 12, 2008).

Iannacone, Laurence. 1975. *Educational policy systems.* Fort Lauderdale, Fl: Nova University Press.

Jarzabkowski, Lucy. 2003. Teacher collegiality in a remote Australian school. *Journal of Research in Rural Education.* Winter. 18, 3. 139-144.

Kane, Pearl. R. 1991. *The first year of teaching. Real world stories from America's teachers.* New York: Walker and Company.

Lee, Jared. 2007. Life after retirement, http://EzineArticles.com/?expert=Jared_Lee. (accessed January 2, 2008).

Littky, Dennis, and Samatha Grabelle. 2004. *The big picture. Education is everyone's business.* Alexandria, VA: Association for Supervision and Curriculum Development.

MacLeod, Jay. 1995. *Ain't no makin' it: Aspirations and attainment in a low-income neighborhood.* Boulder, CO: Westview Press.

Marzano, Robert J. 2007. *The art and science of teaching. A comprehensive framework for effective instruction.* Alexandria, Virginia: Association for Supervision and Curriculum Development.

McDonald, Joseph P. 1992. *Teaching: Making sense of an uncertain craft.* New York: Teachers College Press.

McEwan, Elaine K. 2002. *10 traits of highly effective teachers: How to hire, coach, and mentor successful teachers.* Thousand Oaks, California. Corwin Press, Inc.

Metcalfe, Andrew, and Ann Game. 2006. *Teachers who change lives.* Australia: Melbourne University Press.

Meister, Pamela. 2007. Which came first: The intellectual or the leader? *American Thinker* http://www.american thinker.com/2007/12/which_came_first_the_intellect .html (accessed March 15, 2009).

Mezirow, Jack. 1991. *Transformative dimensions of adult learning.* San Francisco, CA: Jossey-Bass.

Moir, Ellen. 2004. Phases of first year teaching. *New mentor Training Program 2004-2005.* Greece Central School District. www.greeceK12.ny.us

Nieto, Sonia. 2003. *What keeps teachers going?* New York: Teachers College Press.

Nye, Barbara, Spyros Konstantopoulos, and Larry V. Hedges. 1991. How large are teacher effects? *Education Evaluation and Policy Analysis,* 26, 3:237–257.

Olsen, Brad, and Dena Sexton. 2009. Threat rigidity, school reform, and how teachers view their work inside current education policy contexts. *American Educational Research Journal* 46, 1:9–44.

Payne, Ruby. 1998. *A framework for understanding poverty.* Highlands, TX: RFT Publishing Co.

Perkinson, J. Henry. 1977. *The imperfect panacea. American faith in education, 1865-1976.* New York: Random House.

Reynolds, Susan. 2008. *My teacher is my hero.* Avon, Massachusetts: Adamsmedia.

Teddlie, Charles, and David Reynolds. 2000. Linking school effectiveness and school improvement. In *The international handbook of school effectiveness research,* ed. Charles Teddlie and David Reynolds. New York: Falmer Press.

Reynold, Anne. 1992. What is competent beginning teaching? A review of the literature. *Review of Educational Research* 62,1:1–35.

Savonmaki, Pasi. 2005. Collaboration among teachers in polytechnics. *New Zealand Journal of Teachers' Work 2,* 2:152–155.

Shulman, Lee S. 1987. Knowledge and teaching: Foundations of the new reform. *Harvard Educational Review* 57, 1:1–22.

Spring, Joel. 1976. *The sorting machine. National education policy since 1945.* New York: Longman.

Staw, Barry, Llyod E. Sandelands and Jane Dutton. 1981. Threat rigidity effects in organizational behavior: A multilevel analysis. *Administrative Science Quarterly* 26: 501–524.

Traina, Richard P. What makes a good teacher, www.educationweek.org. (accessed January 7, 2008).

Willms, Douglas J. 1992. *Monitoring school performance: A guide for educators.* Washington, DC: Famler Press.

Yell, Mitchell & Erik Drasgow. 2005. *No child left behind. A guide for professionals.* Upper Saddle River, NJ: Pearson.

Index

Teachers' Choice, 80
teaching: assignments in uptown
    New York, 78–79; circle, 40–41;
    competency defined, 9; definition,
    120; as a dialectical process, 7; first
    year, 19–32; is emotional, 121; is
    physical, 121; last year, 101–9; as a
    political act, 7
teaching after retirement, 115–16; re-
    teaching daughter, 111–12; teaching
    quilting, 115
teaching/research, 100
"Teach Tolerance," 77
teach to the test, 128
Teddlie and Reynolds, 6–7
third-grade students, growth of, 105
threat rigidity theory, viii
Three Billy Goats Gruff lesson, 88

tolerance as racism, 77
Traina, Richard, 3

United Federation of Teachers, 80
uptown New York, 78–79

village, classroom as, 47

Warner, Sylvia Ashton, 95
Weber, Lillian, 23–24
Westside Preparatory School, 2–3
what worked, 64–65
Wilder, Laurie Ingalls, 56
Willms, Douglas J., 6
"Word Walls," 48
writing project (Caulkin), 86–87

"Yes We Can!" 81

Breinigsville, PA USA
08 September 2010
245004BV00001B/3/P